Come to me, all who labor and are heavy laden, and I will give you rest. Take my yoke upon you, and learn from me; for I am gentle and lowly in heart, and you will find rest for your souls. For my yoke is easy, and my burden is light.

Matthew 11:28-30

For now we see in a mirror dimly . . .

1 Corinthians 13:12a

The Yoke of Jesus

A School for the Soul in Solitude

ADDISON HODGES HART

William B. Eerdmans Publishing Company

Grand Rapids, Michigan / Cambridge, U.K.

Published 2010 by
Wm. B. Eerdmans Publishing Co.
2140 Oak Industrial Drive N.E., Grand Rapids, Michigan 49505 /
P.O. Box 163, Cambridge CB3 9PU U.K.
www.eerdmans.com

Printed in the United States of America

16 15 14 13 12 11 10   7 6 5 4 3 2 1

Library of Congress Cataloging-in-Publication Data

Hart, Addison Hodges, 1956-
The yoke of Jesus: a school for the soul in solitude /
Addison Hodges Hart.
p.   cm.
ISBN 978-0-8028-6510-6 (pbk.: alk. paper)
1. Spirituality. 2. Spiritual life — Christianity.   I. Title.

BV4501.3.H376   2010

248 — dc22

2009043728

Contents

CONTENTS

chapter 1

INTRODUCTION
A School for the Soul in Solitude

Religion is what the individual does with his own solitariness.

A. N. Whitehead,
Religion in the Making

The core of the soul is sensitive to nothing but the divine Being, unmediated. Here God enters the soul with all he has and not in part, and nothing may touch that core except God himself.

Meister Eckhart, *Sermons,* 1

I magine yourself in a dark wood. Not only that, but imagine that this dark wood is all that you know —

indeed, the only environment you have ever known. Imagine, further, that the canopy of branches above you is so thick with leaves and festooned with vines and hanging mosses that the sky has never been visible to you. You have no idea of what the sun in its direct brilliance looks like. The moon and the stars are luminaries you have never seen. The dome of heaven is veiled, and any notion of a vast expanse of space beyond this world is likewise beyond your comprehension.

I use this image to suggest the confining mental limitations of the world in which we actually find ourselves. That which blocks out the sunlight and starlight in our experience is not the trees of a forest, but the surroundings of our man-made environment. The heavens above us are more likely to go unnoticed because of the skyscrapers or the billboards or the television or the computer screen before our eyes. The man-made world is firstly an *inner* condition, a downright soul-sickness, a delusion that begins in the human imagination. From there, "from within, out of the heart of men," it becomes concrete; so much so that the modern secular city may well be, with its temples built in homage to commerce, the *exteriorization* of our civilization's "collective soul." Nature is pushed aside by the enormous and the sprawling, obscured by detritus and the absurdly ugly; and then, wrapped round all that, are serpentine highways congested with tiny fuming wheeled boxes; and finally come the larger domestic boxes of the suburbs and the many square miles of shopping centers pushing ever outward into the surrounding landscape far and wide.

Along with the ravages of secular ugliness, what is often intentionally blotted from sight and hearing in our civilization are the expressions of humanity's *religious mind.* In other words, what has ever been the heart and soul of culture — the origin and sustainer of philosophy, arts, ethics, and virtually everything else that opens up human existence to its sacred dimension — is being displaced by the profane and the tawdry so rapidly that we scarce can take it in. Those things that are good, beautiful, and true have never been under such relentless siege as they are in the modern world.

However, the tension between the man-made "world" — the world of illusion made concrete — and the religious mind behind all humanity's great traditions is not a new development. In Christian language, when the word *world (kosmos)* is used in its negative sense, it means precisely the man-made civilization that makes tangible the interior rejection of the spiritual dimension. St. Augustine famously used the analogy of two cities to describe this inner struggle of man's condition, a cleavage that runs not only through every civilization, but also through each human soul. When this condition is described at the level of the individual soul, it is called in the Epistle of James "double-minded" (literally, *dipsychoi* — "two-souled ones"; James 1:8 and 4:8). St. Augustine, referring to the same condition on the collective, civilizational level, wrote, "Accordingly, two cities have been formed by two loves: the earthly by the love of self, even to the contempt of God; the heavenly by the love of God, even to the contempt of self."[1]

Augustine's "earthly city" is what the New Testament means by "the world," and the First Epistle of John *defines* the world in this manner: "Do not love the world or the things in the world. If any one loves the world, love for the Father is not in him. For all that is in the world, the lust of the flesh and the lust of the

1. Augustine, *The City of God,* Book XIV, chap. xxviii.

eyes and the pride of life, is not of the Father but is of the world" (1 John 2:15-16).

These three aspects of human civilization divorced from God and the perennial religious mind are, then, the following: *sexual lust,* whereby one person is objectified, depersonalized, and viewed as existing solely for another person's gratification ("lust of the flesh," which is the opposite always of a self-giving exchange of love); *avarice* or *greed* or mere *acquisitiveness* ("lust of the eyes"); and *hubris* or *arrogance,* possibly meaning of a national or ethnic nature, as exemplified and promoted by all the empires and governments of the world in every age ("pride of life").

If one pauses for a moment to reflect on this program by which the world's agenda is recognized, one rather quickly notices that not a lot has changed since this deft analysis. In fact, we might perhaps see these three things far more starkly and rudely in our present day than ever before. They constitute our cultural identity to a gigantic extent. What should scare us, if we have even a smidgen of religious consciousness, is that it has grown so gigantic that all too often we no longer even notice it. It is more and more like a dark wood we have always lived in, insensible to what lies beyond.

5

The way out of our man-made dark wood is, for each of us, a solitary venture and a necessary one.

First, we must decide that we need to go beyond it and embrace a larger reality than the one to which we have become accustomed. Then, we must begin the daunting task of doing what needs to be done. To do this could mean that we put resolutely behind us pestering voices that would tell us of the futility or idiocy of such a pursuit. There will always be those who will insist — for reasons of "practicality" or "science" or "progress" or "national interest" or "civic duty" or "family responsibility" or whatever else can be conjured up — that the dark wood is all there is and all that matters and all that *should* matter to *us.* But we should stubbornly and rebelliously put our packs on our backs and move on anyway. We travel with others who have made and are making the same spiritual journey, but it's going to be our own two legs — actually, our own *minds* — that will carry the weight of the journey.

I'm reminded of someone who long ago described himself as being in a similar dark wood and pursued by three wild beasts. Dante Alighieri begins the very first canto of his *Divine Comedy* in this way:

Midway upon the journey of our life
I found myself in a dark wilderness,
for I had wandered from the straight and true.[2]

The three beasts that hem him in and frighten him are a leopard, a lion, and a she-wolf (cf. Jer. 5:6). Respectively, taken in the moral sense, these represent lust, pride, and avarice — those same three marks of man's delusional world as listed by St. John. What the three beasts symbolize reappear in numerous forms throughout the first two parts of the *Commedia,* first in their final consequences for the human soul if they remain unchanged by the grace of God *(Inferno),* and then in their purgation as the soul is transformed through repentance and absolution *(Purgatorio).*

Dante's journey is a solitary one, even though he is guided by Virgil, then his beloved Beatrice, and finally St. Bernard of Clairvaux. The three beasts of the dark wood are both external to him and, as the *Purgatorio* makes evident, internal to him. Dante must move from the divided condition within his own soul, ceasing to be "double-minded," and progressively come

2. Dante Alighieri, *Inferno,* trans. Anthony Esolen (New York: Modern Library, 2005), ll. 1-3.

to possess "singleness of vision" — which means "to seek first the Kingdom of God" (see Matt. 6:22-24 and 33, KJV, wherein Jesus says that the eye must be *"single"* — in Greek, *haplous;* this refers to the *single-minded* focus necessary for apprehending God and his righteousness).

The point is this: the way out of the dark wood requires personal solitary effort. The man-made forest is all around us. The beasts are both outside and within. And, if we want to know for ourselves the truth of sages and mystics down the ages, we need to undertake the journey personally. We also need to be transformed and purged from the world's illusions — that is to say, from lust, avarice, and pride in all their multifarious shapes.

This endeavor is, to be sure, the primary purpose of "private prayer." It is a frequently overlooked fact that every time Jesus' teachings on the practice of prayer are recounted in the Gospels, he speaks of it in its solitary mode. Likewise, with only a few exceptions, when he is depicted at prayer, he has gone off apart to be alone. Private, solitary prayer is essential if we are to "know" God and be transfigured by the encounter. Jesus firmly commands each follower of his, "But when you pray, go into your room and shut the door and pray to your Father who is in secret; and your Father who sees in secret will reward you" (Matt. 6:6). So crucial is the pursuit of solitary prayer for the Christian disciple that the fourth-century desert father Evagrius of Pontus dared to rephrase Jesus' summons to follow him in this very pointed way: "Go, sell your possessions and give to the poor, and, taking up your cross, deny yourself, so that you can pray [i.e., in solitude] without distraction" (*Chapters on Prayer,* 17).

That we need corporate prayer is not in doubt. The Eucharist above all is a corporate prayer, and it is the heart of the church's life. Yet local churches, especially nowadays in the West, are often not much help in leading their people into the practice of personal prayer. Even when they are not utterly compromised by mundane agenda, trivial activities, politics, or a general loss of the sense of the sacred, modern churches of all stripes are usually more concerned with the social than the personal dimension of religious life. They have a vested interest in promoting the social and the corporate above the private, even to the point of occasionally — and quite wrongly — stressing that the corporate is more important than the personal. In many churches today there can still be heard from the pulpit the dubious notion that "we are not saved individually, but in a body." Well, that may well be true as far as it goes; but the implication that individual prayer is of less value than the corporate is alarmingly at odds with the teachings of Christ. Modern churches do all they can to make the exoteric aspect of Christianity accessible to as many as possible, and do so for a handful of commendable reasons; but the grave loss of the esoteric aspect of prayer, as something both vital and (one might wish) available through practical pastoral teaching, is largely the reason for the spiritually flat, trite, and boring condition that prevails in much church life. This state of affairs really began in the fourth century when the Roman Empire became "Christianized," leading to the proliferation of the monastic life as a way of preserving Christianity's interior core.

Nevertheless, the surprising international popularity of the film *Into Great Silence (Die Grosse Stille),* made by German director Philip Gröning and released in 2006, should remind us that there still exists a desire for the personal and solitary engagement with God as found in the genuine Christian tradition. The movie spends nearly three hours immersing the audience into the life of the Carthusian monks of the Grande Chartreuse in the magnificent French Alps. It is an exquisitely beautiful record of European monastic life, visually stunning and — if one stays with it — profoundly moving. It is to be remembered that the Carthusians are hermits, committed to a life of profound solitude, and gathering only on occasion for liturgy and social interaction.

Interestingly, the film appeared the very year that the "new atheists" (Dawkins, Dennett, Harris, Hitchens, etc.) were beginning to make a media splash with their spate of books. It seems to me that the best rejoinder to their brashness, noise, and "scientistic" chest-thumping was simply the silence and authenticity depicted in this cinematic masterwork. Not an "answer," of course, in the apologetic sense, it is nevertheless powerful visual testimony to something that remains hidden and transcendent throughout the film, veiled just behind the visible activity of monastic prayer. It almost certainly depicts a life beyond the ken of the latest bunch of pop atheists, quietly calling into question the shallowness of their criticisms.

Sadly enough, however, this same religious experience, grown from the careful cultivation of interiority, is frequently unknown to the majority of Christians as well. For one thing, in our loud age of extroversion it is difficult to impress on individual Christians the need for developing the requisite balance of introversion in their lives. Everything in their busy world is geared to distract them from prayer, and distraction — as noted in the quote taken from Evagrius above — has always been the worst danger to developing spiritual awareness, and the first thing warned against by all the great masters of prayer.

And yet *Into Great Silence* was a popular film, and universally well-received by critics who might more typically have been expected to dismiss it. Clearly it "spoke" to viewers, summoning from them the sense of a normally unheeded desire.

THIS IS A ROUNDABOUT WAY of introducing the purpose of this "school for the soul in solitude." Let me explain, then, what this small book is meant to be.

This is a book that provides basic elements of a given subject. It's not an exhaustive text but rather a minimal one, something fundamental. It is focused on the cultivation of one's solitary prayer, and its elements are grouped under a series of subjects that have been ruminated upon and offered for reflection. Perhaps other things and better might have been said about each of the themes addressed. Doubtless many other headings could have been included, but the idea was to keep the book both compact and (one hopes) substantial. It is a book for Christians who are consciously seeking an encounter with the consciousness of God. The whole endeavor of the Christian's spiritual life is to "seek the Lord" in whom we already "live and move and have our being," since he is "not far from each one of us" (Acts 17:27-28). Or, as Rainer Maria Rilke put it, "God is only a direction given to love, not its object."

To explain the book another way, its purpose is to prepare the reader to do something *knowledgeably.* No effort is made to give precise directions or step-by-step details; rather, the goal is to give *ideas* the reader can take and utilize as he or she will. Ideally a school helps one to think for oneself, and it is hoped that this small text will so engage the mind that the reader will have something to ponder in quiet reflection. It is assumed that if one knows *why* this or that aspect of the solitary prayer life is worth doing, then the first steps have thereby already been taken toward incorporating it into one's practice. This requires having some definitions on hand. Understanding is certainly more than definitions, of course, because genuine understanding is based on one's experience. But definitions are necessary, too, and so it is that we are concerned with concepts in this book.

The headings are succinct, sometimes just a single word. They are for the most part progressive in their ordering, though this is not always the case. This text is not a handbook providing methods or techniques. Instead, it is a text that is intended to suggest the concepts that one's own experimentation can shape as it will. Spiritual practice is as individual as the person engaged in it, even if its general elements remain recognizable from one person to the next. As T. H. White had Merlyn say at one point to young Arthur in *The Once and Future King:* "In future you will have to go by yourself. Education is experience, and the essence of experience is self-reliance."[3]

The title of the book, taken from Matthew 11:28-30, is intended to indicate that it is about a "discipline," "discipleship," a way of life. Jesus uses the image of the "yoke" to suggest precisely this: that he has a spiritual discipline to impart to those who wish to follow him.

3. T. H. White, *The Once and Future King* (New York: G. P. Putnam's Sons, 1958), Vol. 1, Chap. 5.

At the end of the day, it is hoped that readers can find here food for thought, encouragement in solitary prayer (sometimes in the face of discouragement), and a motivation to go further.

chapter 2

The Two Goals
and the Long Road Ahead

*Of what avail is it to go across the sea to Christ if
all the time I lose the Christ that is within me
here?*

Leo Tolstoy,
"Two Old Men," *Master and Man*

I f you set out on a long journey for an unfamiliar
destination, it is always advisable to do two things.
First, have an idea of the route you are traveling,
which means possessing a map and a clear set of directions. Second, be willing to ask directions on the
way if you should stray off the beaten path. In short,
know where you're headed (even if it's a place you
have never been and possibly can't even picture to

yourself), and have some idea how to get there (even if the way is itself something of a mystery). Lastly, there is always the fact that the actual experience of the trip will be different than expected. Since it's unforeseeable in its practical daily demands, it's open to all sorts of twists and turns you never saw coming and events you can't control. Thus many carefully laid plans may need to be revised on the spur of the moment, and earlier optimistic imaginings may prove to have been wildly off the mark.

The spiritual life is like that. It is a long journey to a destination that we cannot conceive. It is, in the best sense, existential. This is why we can speak of the way ahead with a certain amount of clear-sightedness, and yet go on to admit that we cannot speak of it adequately at all. No amount of discussion about the subject can amount to the actual experience of prayer. Likewise, everyone's personal experience of prayer will be both like and unlike everyone else's. At some point, one must agree with the sentiment attributed to St. Bernard: "My secret is my own."

This is as it should be. No one is called to know God on behalf of another, and no one else can know God on our behalf. I am not referring here to some kind of relativism, since we are all called to know the same God truly "as he is," and to seek first the same "Kingdom" and "righteousness." Rather, it is only to say that everyone is called to know God for himself or herself; and, because we are unique and unrepeatable persons, we can know God only in relation to the contours of our own particular lives. The bottom line is this: *If* we are to *know* God for ourselves, we really have no choice — no matter how social or small-group-centered or communal or liturgical our religious lives may be in many other respects — but to know him *individually* and *solitarily.* In some ways, the entire Christian community is like the Carthusians in this simple — indeed, unavoidable and existential — feature: it is a *community of solitaries.*

If that sounds extreme, then consider this: we are all existentially "solitary," and we are all ontologically in community as well. That's plainly how it is. The Carthusians live this truth in a particularly extreme mode; but we live it ourselves by the two complementary facts of our *ex-istence* (meaning, quite literally, our personal "standing out from") and simultaneously our *being in solidarity with* the whole human race from its beginning to its end. More than that, Christians realize the sacredness of this solidarity in the sacramental unity of Christ's church, made tangible through our *in-corporation* into the *Corpus Christi,* the Body of Christ, in baptism. The only question, then, applicable both to a Carthusian and to you or me, is merely this: *Are we living into our Christian vocation well or poorly?* That's not to ask whether or not we fail occasionally or fall into sinfulness, whether or not we are imperfect or vulnerable or behave stupidly from time to time, and so on. It's simply to ask whether or not we know where we want to go and the route to get there, whether or not we have a map and are willing to ask for directions in a pinch. "Perfection" is a goal, not a prerequisite. The way ahead is a long road, and a journey is a process (a "procession") — that is to say, it is a course of action, as every process must be. We haven't yet arrived, but — *are we, each one of us, on the road?* What course of action have we adopted, or will we adopt?

Traditionally this course of action, this process, has been called *asceticism,* from the Greek word *askeo* — to "endeavor" or to "do one's best." As a verb the word appears in the New Testament only once, but that single instance has much to tell us about the practical nature of asceticism. Far from being something sensational or self-abusive, which is the commonly held misconception, it is instead quite down-to-earth. In the book of Acts, St. Paul on trial says of his daily practice of religion, "So I always take pains [*asko*] to have a clear conscience toward God and toward men" (Acts 24:16).

From this statement we can note three things about what asceticism meant for Paul. It is, first, *personal effort.* Second, it is primarily concerned with *ethics.* And, third, because Paul *relates it to both God and man,* it is to be seen as a negative way of saying what Jesus had said in positive terms, quoting from the Mosaic Law: "You shall love the Lord your God . . . [and] you shall love your neighbor as yourself." In other words, Christian asceticism means doing one's best to live rightly, loving God and neighbor as Christ commanded. This is what it meant to Paul, and what it has basically meant for Christians in general ever since.

So far, so good. But, as the early Christians already knew, this ethic demanded far more than might appear to be the case. There was a whole regimen to be undertaken, a treatment to undergo, a schema to be adapted to each person's particular set of circumstances. To make the point that the Christian profession was understood as a spiritual way of re-ordering one's entire life, I offer as examples the following mere handful of seemingly straightforward statements drawn from the New Testament.

Jesus taught his followers: "For I tell you, unless your righteousness exceeds that of the scribes and Pharisees, you will never enter the kingdom of heaven" (Matt. 5:20). Something more than outward and conventional law-abiding piety is being insisted upon here.

Saint Paul reminded his readers that the ethics of the Christian are rooted in something more profound than "the written code" or "letter" of the Law; they derive instead from a hidden union with the Spirit (or "Breath") of God: "For the written code kills, but the Spirit gives life. . . . Now the Lord is the Spirit, and where the Spirit of the Lord is, there is freedom. And we all, with unveiled face, beholding the glory of the Lord, are being changed into his likeness from one degree of glory to another; for this comes from the Lord who is the Spirit" (2 Cor. 3:6c, 17-18).

The Second Epistle attributed to St. Peter tells us that "the knowledge of God and of Jesus our Lord" involves an "escape" from "the corruption that is in the world [*kosmos*] because of passion [*epithumia* = passion]," so that we might "become partakers of the divine nature" (2 Peter 1:2, 4). This clearly connects "ethics" to the mystical and the deifying. It also reveals, along with a number of other texts in the New Testament, that what "corrupts" the world God created is something that comes from the disordered condition of man's inner world — the interior turmoil and chaos of "passion" found in every human being.

Turning to the First Epistle of St. John, we find a similar stress on the mystical as the basis for the ethical: "Beloved, we are God's children now; it does not yet appear what we shall be, but we know that when he appears we shall be like him, for we shall see him as he is. And every one who thus hopes in him purifies himself as he is pure" (1 John 3:2-3). In other words, since our goal is to become by grace what God is by nature, our life should be one of self-purification — in other words, asceticism.

These are only a few representative texts. The New Testament is, however, filled with such passages, and only our over-familiarity with them renders us dull to their insistence on the need for each person's intentional and interior transformation. Possibly we hear them so often that we no longer notice them. But, if we look long and hard at them, we will discover afresh that there is a program for our lives that is radical, unsettling, transfiguring, largely esoteric, and focused on clearly transcendent goals.

The desert father Evagrius of Pontus states the New Testament's overall ascetical program in his typical terse style like this: "Love [*agape*] is the offspring of impassibility [*apatheia*], and impassibility is the blossom of asceticism [*askesis*]" (*Praktikos,* 81). Evagrius continues by saying that this involves keeping the commandments of God, which comes ultimately from faith (which he claims is a naturally inherent good that can be found even in those who do not yet believe in God).

Other words for what Evagrius and other spiritual masters mean by *impassibility (apatheia)* are both translated *purity* in English: *hagnos,* as in 1 John 3:3 above, and *katharos,* as in "Blessed are the pure [*katharoi*] in heart, for they shall see God" (Matt. 5:8). The one who hopes to see the Lord and be like him "purifies himself as [the Lord] is pure." To possess *apatheia* is not the same thing as being "apathetic" or cold, lacking compassion and warmth. Quite the opposite, for, as Evagrius says, it results in the capacity to love truly. Impassibility means not being bullied or motivated by one's own disordered passions — such inner things as greed, lust, and pride, with all their "children" — which cause us to be self-seeking and self-gratifying. The real problem you and I must face is not primarily the devil from without, but the passions from within: "What comes out of a man is what defiles a man. For from within, out of the heart of man, come evil thoughts" (Mark 7:20ff.). One who becomes "impassible" is "purified" from giving in to the beguilement of his own evil thoughts. But this takes much time and practice and asceticism.

In short, then, the program is this: If we are to *love* God and man, as Jesus commanded his followers and as Paul confessed to be the purpose of his religious practice, then we must work toward *impassibility,* or *apatheia;* and that means a practical *asceticism* focused on the ethics of the Kingdom and God's righteousness (Matt. 6:33).

Christians of the earliest centuries regarded this ethical and mystical program simply as their *philosophy* ("love of wisdom"). In an age when religion and philosophy were not yet distinct, and all the ancient philosophical schools were concerned with how one sought "the good life" or the life of virtue, the Christians' philosophy was reflected in their lives of sincere asceticism — their living, that is, according to the program laid down by the incarnate Wisdom of God, Jesus, through his apostles and teachers.

Christianity was a wholly integrated way of life, not merely a body of abstract doctrines, sliced ever thinner, to which one gave mere intellectual assent or passable lip-service. Let me illustrate this fact with one glaring example. In stark contrast to later Christians and the dismal record of later centuries, no Christian of the first three centuries could have been anything but shocked and scandalized by the abhorrent idea of doing violence to another human being for the sake of Christ or for the preservation of "orthodox belief." The church's orthopraxy — the right practice of living life according to Jesus — *was* orthodoxy for the early Christians; to *live* it was the true wisdom, the apex of all philosophy. The early Christians, not to put too fine a point on it, actually took the Sermon on the Mount at face value and sought to implement it.

SO, THEN, THERE ARE TWO evident goals in the Christian life. One is immediate and the other is the long-range consequence of the first, and to achieve both of these goals one must do one's best in the practice of asceticism. These two goals are spelled out clearly in the very first of the *Conferences* of

25

St. John Cassian (c. 360-430), who traveled to Egypt along with his friend, Germanus, to learn the tradition of asceticism from the desert fathers. As the age of Constantine and his heirs got underway and began to blur the crucial distinction between Christ's church and Caesar's empire, this tradition was kept flourishing among the hermits and monasteries in the deserts of Egypt and Palestine. The first conference that Cassian relates is a dialogue with Abba Moses, who explains to the two visitors the difference between *scopos* and *telos* in the spiritual life.

The *scopos* is the immediate goal one strives to master in order to achieve the *telos* — the ultimate end of a set course of action. All the arts and disciplines have these two goals, says Abba Moses, and he uses various analogies to illustrate his point. The farmer works hard on preparing and maintaining his fields, and that's his immediate goal or *scopos.* His ultimate aim — or *telos* — is to have an abundant crop for the sake of life and prosperity. Another of Moses' images is that of the archer who seeks the prize at an archery contest. The archer's *telos* is to win the prize; his *scopos* is gaining sufficient skill to hit the bull's-eye. Moses goes on to say that, unless the *scopos* is clearly set and understood, the *telos* might never be

26

achieved: thus, if one removes from the archer's viewpoint the target at which he must aim, no amount of wild shooting into the air will win him the prize.

So it is, too, with the spiritual life. The *telos,* the ultimate end, Abba Moses tells Cassian and Germanus, is the Kingdom of God or eternal life. It is also, as 1 John 3:2-3 and Matthew 5:8 put it, "seeing" the Lord, and thus becoming "like him." The immediate aim, the *scopos,* is "purity of heart" and "holiness." Moses cites Romans 6:22 ("hav[ing] your fruit unto holiness, and the end everlasting life," KJV) and Philippians 3:13-14 ("forgetting those things which are behind, and reaching forth unto those things which are before, I press toward the mark [*kata scopon dioko*] for the prize of the high calling of God"). Abba Moses insists that "purity of heart," then, because it is the *immediate* goal, must be the fixed focus of all our attention in asceticism, just as surely as the fixed point of the target's bull's-eye must be the aim of the practicing archer. He must be able to see the target before him and stay clearly focused on it. If he becomes distracted from the immediate goal of perfecting his aim, the ultimate goal of the prize will not be his. "Whatever can guide us," says Abba Moses to his friends, "towards this *scopos,* which is purity of heart, is to be pursued with all our power; but whatever draws us away from it is to be avoided as dangerous and harmful."

THE REMAINDER OF THIS BOOK is about our immediate aim, our *scopos.* Christian life, which is essentially the life of prayer coupled with right action, involves asceticism. Asceticism, in turn, is seeing both our goals, the immediate and the ultimate, and then focusing our efforts on the immediate. Seeking purity of heart, becoming progressively free from the chaos and bullying of our inner passions, and endeavoring to love God and neighbor according to the way of Christ: these are our philosophy, our orthopraxy, and our *scopos.* By focusing pragmatically on the immediate goal, we see what inner resources we already have or don't have, what we should endeavor to acquire in the way of knowledge and experience, and what realistically can be done within our immediate context. We trust that our ultimate destiny is in the hands of God, so we needn't be concerned with that directly. We should instead follow Christ in the immediacy of our own daily circumstances, and that is precisely the frame of mind that Jesus calls all his disciples to have. One need only consult the Sermon on the Mount to see the truth of that rather clearly.

The Two Goals and the Long Road Ahead

What we now turn to in the chapters that follow are some components of our tradition to reflect upon, and some practical implements to utilize, to help us along in the direction of our immediate aims. Each of these components has real utility for our discipleship — they are the stuff from which the "yoke" of Jesus is made. Whether they appear at first to be abstract notions (for example, "faith"), or something to contemplate (for example, "nature"), or something to do (for example, "reading"), they all have practical value for us. Indeed, there is nothing more practical, yet more personally enriching, than the daily routines and disciplines of the Christian's life. One can be certain that if something is impractical or purely theoretical in nature, it has very little to do with genuine Christian living.

chapter 3

Faith

The righteous shall live by his faith.

Habakkuk 2:4

Once while teaching on the subject of prayer, Jesus put this hard and difficult question to his disciples: "When the Son of man comes, will he find faith on earth?" (Luke 18:8b). There is something being suggested in this simple query that is troubling, mainly because of the identity of the one posing it. Surely — if Jesus himself didn't provide the answer — then something challenging indeed is being put before us and before every generation of Christ's followers. That Jesus said this in the context of an instructive parable he told for the purpose of underscoring "that men ought always to pray, and not to faint" (Luke 18:1, KJV) is a reminder to us that prayer is the primary — and a permanent — expression of religious faith.

So much has been said and written about faith that it seems that to say more about it is superfluous. Still, while acknowledging this caveat, we know that Jesus' sharp-edged question remains before us, and that there is no more important place to begin when addressing the Christian's interior life than faith. It is unquestionably where everything else finds its source, the hidden origin of both knowledge and longing; and it is experienced, as St. John of the Cross put it, in "the night" — that is to say, in obscurity and from a place within that precedes our conscious awareness. This is what is meant when Hebrews 11:1 (KJV) says of faith that it "is the substance of things hoped for, the evidence [or, conviction] of things *not seen*" (emphasis mine). This particular biblical text, so often quoted as a "definition" of faith, is more accurately a statement of what faith accomplishes in a person: it generates awareness and ultimately an experiential knowledge of things not immediately apparent to the senses, but felt to be real nonetheless.

There is a common misconception that faith is irrational, and frequently it is contrasted to "knowledge." Indeed, if what we mean by "knowledge" is only that about which we can reason based on the empirical, as derived from sensual experience alone, then "faith" is clearly not that. Rather, faith is the driving force that must precede and motivate every act of "reasoning" whatsoever — it's the reason we reason about things at all. St. Anselm's famous aphorism regarding theology, that it is *fides quaerens intellectum* — "faith seeking understanding" — might well be said of the pursuit of any form of human knowledge. Evagrius of Pontus, we may recall from the last chapter, regarded faith as an inherent human good, something which doesn't necessitate direct reference to God. I would add that it needn't be outwardly "religious" in any way generally thought of as such; instead, it is the precondition for the uniquely human desire to know, explore, search out, invent, create, and document. Without it, we would be no different than the other animals. It's primarily faith, not reason (which is only an aspect or offshoot of faith), that sets us apart as a species. Faith is what Einstein actually was expressing when he said, "The most incomprehensible thing about the universe is that it is comprehensible." It may even be true to say that faith in this sense best indicates what it means to be "made in the image of God": the peculiar, amphibious quality unique to man to stand both inside and — intellectually and imaginatively — outside his own given, natural context.

The word *faith* means "trust," and it is a profound trust that *things make sense,* that there is coherence and indeed beauty in the world, and that there is — further — a truth and a meaning that can be sensed in all that exists, something that can be called *sacred,* that informs the human consciousness and presses it to understand. Faith points us in the direction of the sacred like the needle of a compass points us toward the north. Even the "cold rigors" of science are, at their purest, a striving toward the sacred. It's only "scientism" that threatens to undermine this simple, basically irrefutable fact. On one level, then, and certainly on a level that pertains to the matter of prayer, Jesus' question might mean something like, "When the Son of man comes, will he find among human beings some lingering sense of, or striving after, the sacred?"

That is a question well worth pondering in today's world. The industrial and technological age has done us no favors in this regard. Increasingly, with our myriad distractions, our heads wired individually in intentional isolation to our own industrial-strength music, with useless "information" politically pumped into our minds by talking — frequently yelling — heads, our imaginations teeming with the "entertainment" of fast-moving violence or coarse sexuality, it is no wonder that the sacred seems somehow nonexistent to us.

We have desacralized our culture. When there is no "cult" left, there essentially is no culture left either, and where there is no culture, there is arguably no genuine humanity. The virtues can be forgotten, humaneness can be dispensed with, and "information" can take the place of traditional "in-formation" — that is to say, the full formation of the human soul. In only a very short space of time in the whole, vastly longer history of mankind, we have managed to create an anthropocentric, technologically "virtual" world that insulates us from direct interaction with reality. By "reality" I mean the obvious sense of the sacred that every preceding generation of man sensed in the mysterious universe around it. It is Augustine's "earthly city" in a form more horrific than anything he could have imagined. The truth is, we don't need any more dystopias imagined for us by the likes of Orwell or Huxley or a thousand other fiction writers; we live every day in a massive dystopia already. So, again, "When the Son of man comes, will he find among human beings some lingering sense of, or striving after, the sacred?"

The sort of faith, though, that we are to emulate as followers of Christ is both a sense of the sacred, even in the midst of the world's distractions, and something even more specific. It is the faith of Abraham, as St. Paul stresses in Romans 4 and Galatians 3 and 4. It is trust in God himself, trust in his calling and promises, and trust that he will take us where we should go.

It is interesting to note the place where Abraham — or Abram, as he was first called — appears in the Bible. The first eleven chapters of Genesis tell the story of mankind as a series of failures: Adam and Eve's loss of Paradise, then the murder of Abel by his brother Cain, then the first city built by the first murderer, then the increase of violence and the judgment of the Flood, and then the hubris of the "technological" civilization of Babel seeking to unseat God. God repeatedly shows severity and mercy, but nothing ultimately works to bring man back to his senses. These stories are to be seen not so much as literal history as paradigms of mankind's "loss" of what it means to be human. As the Greek fathers of the church and the Cistercian fathers of the twelfth century sometimes expressed it, man has retained God's "image" but lost — and must recover — his "likeness." It is at this point, in Genesis 11, following the string of paradigmatic human failures, that we first meet Abraham.

In the story the Lord merely calls Abraham to follow him: "Go from your country and your kindred and your father's house to the land that I will show you" (Gen. 12:1). The call of Abraham is a new beginning, a new way that God will deal with the human race. It is the way of faith, of personal trust in following the Lord wherever he leads the person willing to go. There are no guarantees made to Abraham himself, only a grand promise that God will bless his faith with a remarkable fecundity in the ages to come. His own life will have its ups and downs and even one especially hard moment of testing (Gen. 22!), but through it all Abraham is to walk with his Lord. In Chapter 15, in a passage taken up by Paul to reveal how God justifies us all by faith, we read this of Abraham: "And [Abraham] believed the LORD; and [the LORD] reckoned it to [Abraham] as righteousness" (Gen. 15:6). It is in this personal interaction between Abraham and the Lord that we see the specific nature of the faith that Jesus is ultimately referring to when he asks his disciples his very difficult question. Will the Son of man find this sort of faith — faith as pure as Abraham's — on the earth when he comes?

There is no doubt that Jesus' calling of his disciples to leave all and follow him was meant to be a call to faith as radical as the summons God issued to Abraham in Genesis. For example: "Foxes have holes, and birds of the air have nests; but the Son of man has nowhere to lay his head. . . . No one who puts his hand to the plow and looks back is fit for the kingdom of God" (Luke 9:58, 62). The parallel is intentional, as is Jesus' frequent statement to those he healed and absolved of sin: "Your faith has saved you."

We see the emphasis on Abraham's faith in numerous contexts, usually implicit, but occasionally it is explicitly stated by Jesus. On one occasion he says of the woman he heals in the synagogue on the Sabbath, who had been deformed by "a spirit of infirmity": "And ought not this woman, *a daughter of Abraham* whom Satan bound for eighteen years, be loosed from this bond on the sabbath day?" (Luke 13:16, emphasis mine). In another place, when Zacchaeus, the undersized tax collector, has exhibited his repentance and faith by showing what pains he would take to make amends for his former greed and extortion, Jesus says to the crowd, "Today salvation has come to this house, *since he also is a son of Abraham*" (Luke 19:9, emphasis mine). Jesus is not referring at all to their ethnicity when he refers to these two persons as a "daughter" and a "son" of Abraham. He speaks to them as spiritual heirs of Abraham, a possibility openly extended to all peoples. As God promised Abraham in Genesis, "In [you] shall *all families of the earth* be blessed" (Gen. 12:3, KJV). Restoration of the whole human condition is promised to those "who also walk in the steps of that faith of our father Abraham" (Rom. 4:12, KJV). And, as Paul also writes, "Thus Abraham 'believed God, and it was reckoned to him as righteousness.' So you see that it is men of faith who are the sons of Abraham. . . . For as many of you as were baptized into Christ have put on Christ. There is neither Jew nor Greek, there is neither slave nor free, there is neither male nor female; for you are all one in Christ Jesus" (Gal. 3:6-7, 27-28).

Coming back, then, to prayer: faith as personal trust in God and following Jesus wherever he leads is the sole basis of it. Our intention, as with Abraham and Christ's first disciples, must simply be to go with him, even to the forsaking of other things. Prayer is the context in which we withdraw ourselves from the many distractions of many voices and many demands, to listen and converse with the Lord. It is the place where the constant buzz of useless information is replaced with the essential *in-formation* of the Spirit. It is where we can recover the proper consciousness of the sacred and — more than that — "walk" with the Lord.

Finally, faith involves work. Once, when Jesus was asked, "What must we do, to be doing the works of God?" he answered by saying, "This is the work of God, that you believe in him whom [God] has sent" (John 6:28-29). We have come back, then, to the theme of the ascetical life, the living out of our discipleship; and it begins when we do the difficult work — seemingly quite difficult in our day and age — of shutting our doors and learning to pray in faith to our Father in secret (Matt. 6:6). At the end of the day, Jesus' difficult question — "When the Son of man comes, will he find faith on earth?" — finds the beginning of an answer right here and from each one of us individually.

chapter 4

·················

Separation

*Love consists in this, that two solitudes protect
and border and salute each other.*

Rainer Maria Rilke,
Letters to a Young Poet

O ne of the aspects of Christ's call to us to follow
him that is often downplayed is his insistence
on separation and detachment. This is not a call re-
served for the clergy or for monks. It is for his *disciples,* of which number we are all included by virtue of
faith and baptism. Indeed, the much later and dubious distinction made between "religious vocation"
and the "secular life of the laity" simply wasn't part of
Jesus' original message at all. Faith in Christ, mod-

eled on the faith of Abraham, as we have seen, is a call to the individual person to be radically related to God and his Kingdom.

The personal Christian commitment for the earliest generations of the church involved a conscious re-ordering of one's perception of self, family, and society. It was a re-ordering that stood in contrast to the ethos of the world surrounding it, an inversion of the general societal agenda. In Greco-Roman culture, the ordered and stratified social obligations were expected to take precedence over the life of the family, and in turn the family was viewed as having more importance (and greater social benefit) than the individual person.

Christianity inverted that pyramid of the status quo, at least up until the time when the Empire was "Christianized" and Christianity's residual revolutionary potential was consequently tamed. Government and society were not condemned by Christian apostles and apologists, but were seen as providing a safe place for the much more important (because instituted by God at the creation) association of the family. Thus St. Paul could write to Christians living in the capital city, before the persecutions under Nero,

> For rulers are not a terror to good conduct, but to bad. Would you have no fear of him who is in authority? Then do what is good, and you will receive his approval, for he is God's servant for your good. But if you do wrong, be afraid, for he does not bear the sword in vain; he is the servant of God to execute his wrath on the wrongdoer. Therefore one must be subject, not only to avoid God's wrath but also for the sake of conscience. (Rom. 13:3-5)

Paul is saying that good government exists to protect and serve life and livelihood, something that, by extrapolation, is expressed by a functioning family unit. In other words, good government exists to serve the needs of human beings — families and individuals.

It's helpful to our understanding to recall that the Roman family was not simply the "nuclear" family we have become accustomed to in recent decades. Traditional in nature, it was often a "compound" operation, intergenerational (as most families throughout history have been), that ran a farm or local trade business or businesses. It involved all family members, as well as slaves if the family was more well-to-do. The family was certainly indebted to the protection provided by the state, and it was praiseworthy only to the extent that it served and supplied that state for the collective good.

Christianity, in subtle contrast to this view, and very clearly Diaspora-Jewish in its thinking along these lines, placed the essential value of the family above that of the state. Judaism had learned from its turbulent history of exile and Gentile conquests to place relatively little trust in rulers. Consequently both Judaism and Christianity held that its adherents should cooperate with the state as long as the latter did not conflict with their allegiance to religion and family.

In the 60s A.D., optimistic trust on the part of Christians in Rome's laws and authority, such as Paul displayed in his earlier letter to the Romans, was seriously eroded once the persecutions began. This is a feature strikingly noticeable in the sheer delight the author of the book of Revelation takes in his (longed for, but historically unrealized) depiction of that city's destruction in Chapters 17 and 18, a text written when — in all likelihood — Domitian, following in the footsteps of Nero, was already heading a second wave of persecution.

CHRISTIANITY CLAIMED the precedence of the family over the state, but Christ himself takes us a step further: the family is of lesser significance than the individual person. After all, families produce *persons* who are answerable to God before all else. In this valuation of the person, Christ created an inversion, one that was not even fully in accord with the norms of Jewish society in his own day, although Judaism has always valued the individual. One cannot help but be struck by the fact that Jesus showed ambivalence about family life, something not very popular to note these days in many conventional contexts, but still it is a fact that can't, and shouldn't, be casually ignored.

On the one hand, all one need do is read Mark 10 to see that Jesus upheld the cause of the family. He upheld marriage. Yet his strict condemnation of divorce was most likely a condemnation of contemporary injustices to women and the inevitable impoverishment that followed their abandonment in Palestinian society. He likewise stood forcefully and repeatedly against the demeaning of children as non-persons, going so far as to make them exemplars of the Kingdom. Alongside these calls for justice and equality, though, we also must place such shocking sayings as these:

If any one comes to me and does not hate his own father and mother and wife and children and brothers and sisters, yes, and even his own life, he cannot be my disciple. (Luke 14:26)

As they were going along the road, a man said to him, "I will follow you wherever you go." And Jesus said to him, "Foxes have holes, and birds of the air have nests; but the Son of man has nowhere to lay his head." To another he said, "Follow me." But he said, "Lord, let me first go and bury my father." But he said to him, "Leave the dead to bury their own dead; but as for you, go and proclaim the kingdom of God." Another said, "I will follow you, Lord; but let me first say farewell to those at my home." Jesus said to him, "No one who puts his hand to the plow and looks back is fit for the kingdom of God." (Luke 9:57-62)

Do you think that I have come to give peace on earth? No, I tell you, but rather division; for henceforth in one house there will be five divided, three against two and two against three; they will be divided, father against son and son against father, mother against daughter and daughter against her mother, mother-in-law against her daughter-in-law and daughter-in-law against her mother-in-law. (Luke 12:51-53)

And Jesus said to them, "The sons of this age marry and are given in marriage; but those who are accounted worthy to attain to that age and to the resurrection from the dead neither marry nor are given in marriage. . . ." (Luke 20:34-35)

The call Jesus makes on individual persons to have an allegiance to him and his cause takes precedence over the claims of both family and society. In our ears these sayings may sound harsh; but then we should not forget that Jesus was a tough, earthy, Middle Eastern man, and his call was initially made to other men of a similar mold.

That women (apparently unattached in at least some cases) were also among his followers and treated with equality is another surprising aspect of both his character and the nature of his call to discipleship (e.g., cf. Luke 8:1-3; 10:38-42). The later stories of St. Thecla and the early virgin martyrs of the Church (Cecilia, Lucy, Agnes, and Agatha being the most famous) all tell of women defying family and society for the cause of Christ — something "simply not done" in cultivated Greco-Roman society. Something radical, both for Jewish and Gentile culture, begins in the call of Jesus to follow him. The emphasis is on the individual, the person, and the call is to be separated and detached in a primary allegiance to him. Maintaining "family values" is not Jesus' first concern, nor is the "improvement" of society. Above everything else, we are to become his followers and "learn from" him how to live our lives, bearing the yoke of discipleship in the midst of the world around us (Matt. 11:29). So, before we consider how his radical demands can be applied to us in our own, quite different context, we should first acknowledge how extreme and revolutionary his original call was.

What is of crucial importance is that Jesus was teaching his disciples a whole new unprecedented way of life. It was, quite simply, "*the* Way," "*the* Kingdom of God." It was to embrace, in the words of T. S. Eliot, "A condition of complete simplicity/(Costing not less than everything)" (*Four Quartets,* "Little Gidding," V). It demanded a cognitive re-orientation, a moral turnaround, a spiritual revolution. This can be immediately grasped by meditating on the Sermon on the Mount, for instance. Therefore, it involved detachment from seeing things in a conventional manner.

Jesus purposely shook up his hearers, a style of teaching fitted to the time and place in which he lived. Exaggeration and hyperbole were tools that the rabbis utilized. We shouldn't be too surprised, therefore, that Jesus could say to his followers that, if they wished to be his disciples, they must "hate" their families and lives, or that "the dead" should be left behind to bury their own dead. That was tough-worded, exaggerated "rabbi talk" for stressing the *urgency* of making new priorities where coming along with him was concerned. In effect he was telling them to drop everything else — at least for the time being — and learn from him *now,* while the opportunity afforded itself. (John's Gospel makes this same urgency explicit, underlining the shortness of Christ's temporal mission, but in very different language: "Yet *a little while* is the light with you. . . . *While* [you] have the light, believe in the light, that [you] may be the children of light"; John 12:35-36, KJV, emphasis mine.) When we read these hard sayings of Christ, we must put them into their cultural context.

But neither should we blunt them and accommodate them too facilely to a comfortable modern lifestyle, taking from them the brick-hardness and verbal pungency they possess. Christ still wants disciples who will place allegiance to him above every other relationship or obligation. Yet, I want to stress that Jesus is concerned to teach us how to live lovingly and rightly with all. *Separation to walk with Christ is intended to transfigure us into those capable of loving others, be they good or evil or just or unjust, just as God does.* This is the whole point of Matthew 5:43-48, for example. The exhortation to become "perfect ones" — *teleioi* — just as "your heavenly Father is perfect" means, in context, to become as "perfect" or "complete" *in love* as God is, who "makes his sun rise on the evil and on the good, and sends rain on the just and on the unjust." We cannot do that if we remain attached to people and situations and institutions that keep us from freely becoming his disciples, and if we are not separated from the world's "way" that distracts us from true spiritual living and the discipline required to learn how to love rightly. There can be no eternal life, no life in the Kingdom, no union with God, if one morally and cognitively is not rescued — "saved" or "healed" — from everything that can potentially destroy that possibility.

So it is that we have more "rabbi talk" of a particularly tough sort: "If your hand causes you to stumble, cut it off. . . . If your foot causes you to stumble, cut it off. . . . If your eye causes you to stumble, tear it out" (Mark 9:43-50, NRSV). Separation here does not mean literal self-mutilation. Rather, as men and women of Jesus' day would have ascertained quite readily, it means severing from ourselves those things we should not handle, those places our feet should not take us, and whatever we should not be taking into our minds and imaginations through our senses. In other words, it is precisely because each human person is of infinite worth to God that we should not entertain those contaminating things that will ruin it.

Perhaps this is what underlies that pithy, possibly authentic saying of Jesus found in the Gospel of Thomas: "Become passers-by" (Logion 42). *Pass by* — don't linger to be tested by those things you would do better to avoid entirely. One finds a similar idea of separation, but in more positive terms, perhaps, in the words spoken during prayer to the desert father Abba Arsenius: "Arsenius, flee, be silent, pray always, for these are the source of sinlessness." Notice that *fleeing* — separating oneself — opens up the possibility for "sinlessness." Indeed, Abba Arsenius had previously prayed to God, saying, "Lord, lead me in the way of salvation," to which the Lord responded, "Arsenius, flee from men and you will be saved."

Separation

Arsenius took this as a call for him to flee to the desert to live a life of permanent separation. Jesus' call to separation need not be so extreme. His own disciples were, after all, sent into the world. They were sent out by him in companies, "two by two," and, after his resurrection, Paul and the other apostles worked with teams of helpers. Separation is not to be confused with isolation; it wasn't that entirely even for the early monks of the desert. Companionship and friendship remain essential to the health of Christian life.

Still, an emphasis is to be placed on the worth of the single person in relationship to God. It is of the highest value, and each man and woman is called by God in Christ to be alone with him often and at his disposal continuously. Even when we find ourselves curious about the relationship of another person with the Lord, Christ sharply brings our attention back to our singular discipleship to him, just as he did with Peter when the latter became too nosey about what was intended in the future for another disciple: "What is that to you? Follow me!" (John 21:22).

So, when we bring it down to our own daily lives, the call to separation, stripped down to its most basic form, is really something simple (but not easy) and twofold (but with many and various possibilities for each individual person).

First, we must practice the asceticism we discussed above, keeping ourselves from those temptations, habits, physical contexts, and perhaps persons that lead us away from Christ. This is as old as Jesus' fundamental teaching about "the two ways" (Matt. 7:13-14).

Second, we need to separate ourselves frequently (flee) so that we can be silent and learn how to pray always. "But when you pray, go into your room and shut the door and pray to your Father who is in secret; and your Father who sees in secret will reward you" (Matt. 6:6).

What St. Antony the Great once said was true for monks is very good advice for us all as we each seek to practice the discipline of separation in order to be apart with God. To maintain our inner peace, he said, "like a fish going towards the sea, we must hurry to reach our cell, for fear that if we delay outside we will lose our interior watchfulness." And Abba Moses adds, "Go, sit in your cell, and your cell will teach you everything."

chapter 5

Stillness

Be still, and know that I am God.

Psalm 46:10

In true silence strength is renewed, and the mind is weaned from all things, save as they may be enjoyed in the Divine will; and a lowliness of outward living, opposite to worldly honor, becomes truly acceptable to us.

John Woolman, *Journal*

Entering our "closet" or "room" or — to borrow monastic language — our "cell" and "shutting the door" means something other than the mere physical act of separating oneself to a literal confined space for time with God. Jesus withdrew to pray solitarily in the wilderness, possibly because — as his parables suggest — he was inwardly nourished by natural surroundings. It is evident that Jesus observed with appreciation birds, flowers, flocks, vines, fish, the sea, day and night. In the Gospels we never see him praying in a "closet," but outdoors. Surely, then, the "closet" of prayer is not a literal bedroom or office or chapel.

Certainly the fathers and spiritual writers down the centuries are correct to see in this exhortation a spiritual withdrawal — what some have referred to as the bringing of the mind into the heart. In other words, to go into one's closet is to go into oneself, to go inward, to what T. S. Eliot calls "the still point of the turning world" (*Four Quartets,* "Burnt Norton," IV). To "shut the door" means to quiet the mind, to "close out" the myriad distractions that would engage us, be they external or internal. It means to turn off the computer and television and cell phone, to take the house phone's receiver off its cradle, to get away from the buzz and hum of "information" (falsely so called) and "news" (which is almost never "new," but only a rehash of the redundant). It is to make our practice of *separation* fruitful through the cultivation of *stillness.*

Stillness aims at silencing the airport terminal and shopping mall inside our heads. Inside we find our minds operating like radios set between broadcast signals, on numerous frequencies simultaneously. We have an endless, jabbering stream of thoughts and half-sentences and advertising jingles, all vying for our attention. On the surface we have ideas, half-baked schemes, incoherent notions, verbal fits and starts, sputtering feelings, ups and downs, unwanted memories, and unruly images. Underneath that we have even deeper nameless dreads, strange desires, longings, yearnings, and a good deal of emotional chaos. Fears of mortality mingle with grocery lists; prices for haircuts jostle with concerns for aging parents; sexual feelings interpenetrate the stressful arithmetic of our financial worries. Our minds are moving constantly, and even our sleep is restless. We will come back to the mind and its thought life, but for now let us concede that what we first must learn to do is *be still.*

Frankly, there is no other way to do this than to observe three practical disciplines.

First, we must practice separation and stillness

daily, and if possible, more than once a day. It must become a habit.

Second, we must practice silence and rhythmic breathing. We will come back to breathing and its significance (and symbolism) in the following two chapters. But here it is enough to note that slowing our breathing also helps us to concentrate our minds. The silence we wish to have is primarily the silencing of our own thoughts and feelings within. As another later chapter will suggest, this can be done with eyes open as well as shut. Observing *nature* — listening to it, breathing it, seeing it, just *taking it in* — has the effect of conveying a certain steadying tranquillity to us. It is God's, and there is nothing more revelatory in our sensory experience than "the book of nature." Creation, like God, has the quality of stillness even in its constant movement and change. Its pace is *real* in a way that the pace of human life *is not.*

The silence should be real silence. No accompanying soft music, as is sometimes done, should be introduced to "get us in the mood," and no "guided meditations" with imaginative exercises should be necessary. These are actually subtle ways to avoid genuine silence, to keep control, to stay in charge. Rather, we must be silent and still, not manipulating our environment with suitable "noise" or manipulated by others' ideas of what we should be picturing in our minds. We should simply be alert for God. A prayer such as the "Jesus Prayer" ("Lord Jesus Christ, have mercy on me") can accompany our breathing in and out, whether spoken softly or repeated in the mind silently, and that will help us focus our attention despite distractions or interior chaos.

Third, we must do this for a substantial length of time. We will not reach any level of inner peace and openness to God if all we practice is a few hasty minutes of sitting down, squeezed between "important" activities. One might as well not bother. We must cut out of our twenty-four hours at least one hour — and, if possible, more than that — for the cultivation of stillness and its offspring, which is true prayer. Prayer is lifting one's self to God. It is an experience of presence, and a profound sensing *in oneself* of the sacred. That requires time and commitment, attention and quiet.

St. Mark the Ascetic (who probably lived in the early fifth century) made this vital observation: "The mind [*nous*] cannot be still unless the body is still also; and the wall between them cannot be demolished without stillness and prayer" (*On Those Who*

Think that They Are Made Righteous by Works, 31;
Philokalia, Vol. I). We will return to the importance of
the "mind" or *nous* in a subsequent chapter, but here
it is enough to say that we are psychosomatic beings,
and we need to keep our bodies still in contemplative
practice in order for our minds to pray as they should.
And it is the mind — not the lips — that is the locus
for real prayer. The mind is what needs to be transformed, and the body needs to be aligned properly
with a mind that has united with Christ's Spirit
through the practice of constant prayerfulness (cf.
1 Cor. 6:17).

SO, WE COME BACK to St. Antony's words quoted at
the conclusion of the last chapter. Most of us are not
monks ("solitary ones") in the classical vocational
sense. Organized monasticism of the ancient and medieval kind is not a necessity except for those who believe themselves called to it; nor can it honestly be
said to be a "higher calling" than that of any of the
baptized. Such sharp "vocational" distinctions, made
in another place and time and without much warrant
apart from their own historical and cultural contexts,
have nothing much to say to us today. But the monastic *witness* of the past and present does have meaning

for us still. All of us are, as we've noted throughout, "monks" or "solitary ones" before God. As such, our personal goal is to establish inner peace in our minds at a level where the chaos is most turbulent. The Spirit of God needs to move over the face of that interior abyss and begin the work of a new creation, bringing out of our personal subconscious swamps and whirlpools an ordered tranquillity. So it is, as we saw above, that "like a fish going towards the sea, we must hurry to reach our cell, for fear that if we delay outside we will lose our interior watchfulness."

We must practice stillness.

chapter 6

Breathing, Existence, and the Spirit

Speak to him thou for He hears,
and Spirit with Spirit can meet —
Closer is He than breathing,
and nearer than hands and feet.

Alfred Tennyson,
The Higher Pantheism, VI

When we become still, as described in the previous chapter, we place our selves in a position to experience our own existence. The simple state of silently and solitarily putting ourselves consciously before God is something we frequently (and for the most part, unconsciously) flee from, because with it, we legitimately fear, may come a crushing sense of

boredom, of meaninglessness, of the roiling distur-
bances within our minds, and so on and so forth.
Stillness and self-awareness in solitude may in effect
cause us even to question what it is that we consider
really to be our *selves.*

The "self" is not what we usually conceive it to be; it
is not to be confused with our "ego," that complex
structure of personal identity necessary for this temporal life we live now — that "I," shaped by our upbring-
ing, culture, religious practice, friendships, and education. Our "selves" are what we are *before* all that and
afterward when we come into eternity, as we are created "in God," the One "in whom we live and move and
have our being." The "self" is what *exists* at our deepest, truest core and will exist — so we hope — forever.

To echo the language of Martin Buber in his small
book *Good and Evil* (a work that has influenced my
own thinking here and in the following chapter), existence is not something we possess or can possess. It
can only be participated in, shared in. True Being is
only, ever on God's side, not ours. As the One who
names himself "I Am," he "alone has immortality and
dwells in unapproachable light" (1 Tim. 6:16). He
alone *possesses* existence. It is his alone as the fully
self-existent Self (the technical theological term for

this is "aseity"); and everything else that exists is contingent on his perfect Being, deriving existence from God's bringing all things — "visible and invisible," in the words of the Creed — out of nothingness.

Our personal existence is a fact, though both it and our "selfhood" come from nothing and are moving still into greater existence. That needs to be stressed, underscored, and understood. Our present existence is a *continuous evolution* from non-existence into a full sharing in complete existence — a participation in the eternal life and divine nature of God himself (cf. 2 Peter 1:4), becoming "like him" (1 John 3:2). Thus, existence for us now is still a *potential,* not a complete actuality. This is also true of our *selves:* "It does not yet appear what we shall be" (1 John 3:2). "For now we see in a mirror dimly, but then face to face" (1 Cor. 13:12).

This is precisely why, at the deepest core of ourselves, we discover in times of stillness that we do not yet know our selves. This can be a very uncomfortable realization at first, and it may remain so until it becomes something we get accustomed to and accept. We realize just how strange and unfamiliar we are to ourselves, ethically, spiritually, emotionally, and otherwise. St. Paul autobiographically referred to such feelings of insecurity surrounding self-identity when he wrote things like the following: "Now I know in part; then [ultimately] I shall understand fully, even as I have been fully understood [by God]" (1 Cor. 13:12). "[Morally] I do not understand my own actions" (Rom. 7:15). "We do not know how to pray as we ought" (Rom. 8:26). Paul was admitting that the encounter with God can be dizzying and disorienting. It is no wonder we sometimes flee stillness, find distractions, and keep ourselves ever on the move. We are running away from the "inconclusive" and all-too-elusive self, holding on to the seemingly more solid ego, and — finding that unsatisfying (because it is itself an insubstantial and constructed form) — looking for something that will keep us preoccupied and stimulated instead. It is also why we so often think, when finally we do stop and think, that everything may actually be *meaningless*.

All of us have the innate predisposition to seek for meaning. We look at this half-baked world ("subjected to futility," as Paul says of it in Romans 8:20), not yet participating in the fullness of existence and still fluctuating between nothingness and ultimate freedom "from bondage to decay" (Rom. 8:21), and we ask if it *means* anything. We look into our own hearts and feel the lack of something immense and elusive and alluring and *missing,* and a longing we can't articulate, and we wonder if that has any *meaning,* either. The short answer is, "It does, but you can't see it *yet.*" Why is that? Because we are still moving from nothingness into true existence and selfhood. Our identities are not the nothingness from which we come, nor are they the constraints and terms and conditions of our egos in this short life, but rather they are the true selves into which we are growing "from one degree of glory to another" (2 Cor. 3:18).

This is what Jesus meant when he said to Nicodemus that "that which is born of the flesh is flesh, but that which is born of the Spirit is spirit" (John 3:6). That which is born of the flesh is "flesh" *only* — it exists in an animal way from conception to natural death, and then it will "perish." That which is born of the Spirit of God is "spirit" — and that means, in John's Gospel, "eternal life" (John 3:16). Again, existence is possessed by God alone, not by us or any created thing. "Flesh" must come and go: that's the ebb and flow of contingent existence, here today and gone tomorrow. But God's life is eternal, continuing forever, and that's what we are called to participate in by virtue of our being made in God's "image and likeness." We are being drawn into a life we cannot comprehend, identities that are to be uplifted and completed in God's own life. We cannot see what the bloom and color of the flower will be when the bud has barely begun to take shape in early spring. Likewise, we cannot know our own eventual glory until the time comes for it to appear.

The great symbol of life in Scripture, as in many traditional cultures, is "breath." In Genesis 2:7 (KJV) we read that "the LORD God formed man of the dust of the ground, and breathed into his nostrils the breath of life; and man became a living soul." Here we have the most basic understanding of both what is meant by "the Holy Spirit" and what is meant by "the soul." The Hebrew for the latter is *nefesh* — which can sometimes be accurately translated as "appetite" or the "throat" as well as "soul." (One can see the earthiness of Hebrew thought in this — nothing "disembodied" and "floating" here.) The word is used throughout the Old Testament, and sometimes it is incorrectly rendered in English translations as "heart." Neither "soul" nor "heart," however, captures the word's essential meaning. *Nefesh* means literally "life breath."

The early Christians understood that when the

Holy Spirit of God ("Holy Breath") is referred to, what is meant is God's very Breath of Life. *Spirit* is so often a word that has been drained of its original import, and along with it such derivatives as "inspired" and "inspiration" have lost their power. Nonetheless, God's "Spirit" means something powerful, almost palpable, dynamic, gusting through human souls and all of creation, and going deep down into and combining with the *nefesh* of the man or woman thirsting for God: "My soul thirsts for thee; my flesh faints for thee" (Ps. 63:1, KJV). When Paul writes that "he who is united to the Lord becomes one spirit with him" (1 Cor. 6:17), he means that we are breathing with the Lord's own *Breath,* as we were meant to do from the beginning of creation. It means that we are moving once again in the direction of complete existence and of our true selves: "And we all . . . are being changed into his likeness from one degree of glory to another; for this comes from the Lord who is the Spirit [Breath]" (2 Cor. 3:18).

This is also why Paul can see that, although we cannot know or understand our selves fully now, and so cannot with any assurance know how to pray unerringly, we can in prayer rely nevertheless on the profound, interior working of the Spirit of God "breathing" at some deep, subliminal level within us: "Likewise the Spirit helps us in our weakness; for we do not know how to pray as we ought, but the Spirit himself intercedes for us with sighs too deep for words. And he who searches the hearts of men knows what is the mind of the Spirit, because the Spirit intercedes for the saints according to the will of God" (Rom. 8:26-27). The "will of God" here has nothing to do, by the way, with God's supposed "plan" for our earthly life. These verses, as they are in context in the eighth chapter of the letter to the Romans, can only refer to the ultimate goal of human existence, which God wills — the perfected life in God.

This is an invitation to find meaning *not* in what has happened to us in our lives, *not* in the identities fashioned for us and by us, but in the existence which we are now sharing in God in Christ, united to his very "life" and "Breath." We cannot know our selves fully yet: "When Christ who is our life appears, then you also will appear with him in glory" (Col. 3:4). Apart from his "glory," then, which has yet to be manifested in us, we are not fully *visible* or *recognizable* even to ourselves. Our *meaning* is still in process, our existence still emerging from nothingness into participation in the divine nature. It will only be seen for what it truly is in the uncreated light of Christ. Then and only then will we be complete and our longing met.

Prayer, then, is learning to *breathe* in God, simply to experience our own *existence* in God, and to keep our *selves* and their *meaning* in him. In the words of the poet Kabir, "He's the very Breath of our breaths." Prayer is never initiated by us, nor is it giving God a list of our wishes and demands, expecting him to respond to us. Prayer is always *our* response to *God.* He speaks first, and we listen: "The words that I have spoken to you are spirit and life" (John 6:63). He *breathes* first, and we learn to *exist* in his presence without flight or self-distraction or dependence on our fleeting, transitory egos. We abide in and find meaning in our *potential,* accepting that this world can never provide sufficient meaning to lives created to be eternal and divine in scope. "Breath," of course, is an analogy of something more transcendent than this ephemeral life can ever provide, but it is a reminder that our existence is a gift and a continuing promise of a potential yet to be realized.

SO, IN PRACTICE, we make ourselves still for a set time before God each day. We slow down, breathing in and out slowly, invoking the name of God. We "imprison" our minds in the words of prayer so that distractions will not carry us off in fantasy or planning or worrying or thinking too much. Perhaps we run beads silently between our fingers to keep our minds focused. We give it time, no rushing off, no busyness. And when, finally, we are just plain "doing nothing," just being, we may begin to see a glimmer of the eternal reality that undergirds all forms of existence, and taste the Sabbath rest of God.

chapter 7
....

The Problem of Evil
and "Unclean Spirits"

The mind is its own place, and in it self
Can make a Heaven of Hell, a Hell of Heaven.

Words ascribed to the devil in
John Milton's *Paradise Lost,* I, l. 254

H aving touched on the meaning of *spirit* and *soul* in Scripture, how these words are related to *breath* and therefore to *life,* we may recall that the New Testament, especially in the Gospels, also refers to "unclean spirits" or "unclean breaths." Sometimes the word *demon* is used instead of "unclean spirit," the former being a word from Greek mythology and folklore, etymologically derived from Sanskrit, and utilized by the writers of the New Testament. The Gospel of Luke even refers in one place to "the spirit of an unclean demon" (4:33), putting together these two synonyms and suggesting that the "demon" in the story has personally *breathed* his uncleanness into the recipient, in this case a man present in a synagogue, presumably there to worship God. By "uncleanness" is meant that impurity which divides a man from unhindered access to God and renders him incapable of breathing in God's "Holy Breath" and life.

"Unclean spirits" are depicted as personal beings, able to act and speak out. For example, the man in the synagogue cries out at Jesus, his voice becoming the vehicle of the spirit who inhabits him: "Ah! What have you to do with us, Jesus of Nazareth? Have you come to destroy us? I know who you are, the Holy One of God" (Luke 4:34). The spirit then bursts into a spasm of violence: he "throws down" the man before coming out of him with no lasting harm done (4:35).

In early Christianity the unclean spirits were understood to be those outside forces that bedeviled human lives with their promptings to do evil. In some cases, just as air is inhaled into the lungs, these "unclean breaths" could be "inhaled" to inhabit the deepest levels of the human soul. In other words, they were external influences on the minds and, consequently, the actions of human beings. Not only was the human psyche affected by these influences, associated in the ancient world with madness and otherwise inexplicable anti-social behavior, but the human body was affected as well. These "unclean breaths" were viewed as sources of physical ailments, as various accounts in the Gospels make evident. The tradition of the desert fathers, following the Middle Eastern belief that the wilderness was particularly haunted by these entities, has it that one of the main purposes of the monk's way of life was to do battle with the demons. In other words, the desert fathers understood themselves as going precisely into the lair of the unclean spirits in order to overcome them within the bounds of their own territory.

If we too quickly dismiss all this as "nothing but" mythology, we will likely miss the essential meaning and truth underlying this idea of combatting personal "unclean breaths" — a meaning which proves to be perennial if examined without literalistic insistence on its ancient conceptual trappings. In the writings of Evagrius of Pontus, to mention once more the most intellectually sophisticated of the desert fathers, we find that the demons or "unclean spirits" are equated with evil "thoughts" *(logismoi),* of which he lists eight in particular: gluttony, impurity (sexual lust), avarice, sadness, anger, *acedia* (i.e., a spiritual malaise that induces one to "give up" on spiritual discipline), vainglory, and pride (*Praktikos,* 6). Whether or not his list of evil thoughts is exhaustive or requires any adjustment is beside the point. What should be noted here is that, in line with Evagrius's teaching, "unclean breaths" are (personalized) "ideas" or "thoughts" that are blowing about in the world's atmosphere, so to speak, and they influence from outside the imagination, the emotions, and the reasoning of human minds. That they possess a "personal" nature is certainly a valid way of perceiving them — "mythological" or not, the notion of a "personal" aspect of evil has much to teach us. "Unclean breaths" can be understood as being "in the air," engendered or furthered by human or preternatural minds and passed from one imagination to another, as subtly infectious as disease that is borne by breath. When those "breaths" become our breaths, when our inner imaginations and reasoning conceive actions, then these spirits *possess us* and truly are *personally* incarnated. They can then go on, through word and deed, to poison the souls of others, too.

Evil is something that the Scriptures do not seek to explain. (The Bible is — in anachronistic philosophical terminology — "existential" in nature, not a work of scholastic theology.) It is perhaps of interest here for us to go back to the beginning in reflecting biblically on the nature of evil, quite literally back to the book of Genesis. What does it mean when Genesis 3 tells us in profound mythological language that Adam and Eve partook of the fruit of the tree of "the knowledge of good and evil"?

We should not be at all surprised by the fact that the *only* way the mystery of evil can be discussed is through the inspired medium of myth and fable. Evil is not primarily a philosophical, psychological, or sociological problem; it precedes all such human disciplines and treatments, which can only assume the existence of evil and not explain it. Similarly, there can be no "historical" or "scientific" explanation, since the latter can only investigate certain facts and records relating to the human condition. Because evil is an ontological category, it can most adequately be addressed by the mythological, since myth poetically, and thus more truthfully, reflects what is and simultaneously what defies rational explanation. In fact, the point to grasp here is that "the knowledge of good and evil" is something which only God *can* handle and understand, because he transcends it. We can only get at it through the medium of the collective dream-story, and that is what we mean by myth. It is truth conveyed at the most profound and subliminal level of being.

When the Bible uses the term "to know," it doesn't mean by that an abstract knowledge. Abstraction is a Greek tendency of thought, not a Hebrew one (though, of course, such a neat categorizing of the differences isn't to be pressed too far!). What is primarily meant in Hebrew thought by "knowledge" is "direct experience."

To take one example, often obscured in modern English translations, when sexual intercourse is referred to, the Hebrew says that so-and-so "knew" his wife: "Now Adam knew Eve his wife, and she conceived and bore Cain" (Gen. 4:1). This is also the sense of "knowledge" when Genesis 3 speaks of "the knowledge of good and evil": man was not intended to *experience directly* what he could not handle, what only God can circumscribe by virtue of his eternal and transcendent nature. God alone has power over chaos and order, nonexistence and existence, the unformed and the formed, the underworld and the heights; he alone transcends all categories, and — because he brings all things out of nothing — he governs the forces of unfolding being and life and also the opposing chaotic tendencies that are pulling back toward nonbeing and catastrophe. He embraces time, space, nature — all the powers that man finds unruly and inexplicable. When man, within "spacetime" and subject to the direct experience of "good and evil," stands baffled before the breathtaking beauty and the wildness and ferocity of nature, when he sees that he loves the creation but also fears its unpredictability and violence, he stands before that which he cannot (yet) comprehend, unable to perceive "the big picture" that God perceives from his eternal perspective. The irony of Genesis 3 is that man thinks he can "become like God" only because he has plunged himself unprepared into an experience that he was meant to be protected from and ultimately to transcend. When God banishes Adam and Eve from Eden and the tree of life, because "the man has become like one of us, knowing good and evil" (3:22ff.), it is both a sign of his mercy and a statement of irony. Man is not like God; instead, he is victim of the forces he thought he could handle.

The story of the Sorcerer's Apprentice, familiar to us through the version in the 1940 Disney film *Fantasia* and the tone poem of Paul Dukas, comes close to the idea here. The apprentice tries to imitate his sorcerer-master's powers in the latter's absence. One may recall the iconic image of Mickey Mouse in sorcerer's robes and hat too large for him, brandishing the magician's wand and making an utter shambles of everything around him. When the sorcerer returns, he puts things back to rights, and the apprentice is humbled into realizing that he tried to manage what he was not ready to tackle. He attempted to wield the full power and authority of the one who knows how to handle the magic. He does indeed have a direct experience of magic — as man unfortunately does of good and evil — but such knowledge is beyond his comprehension, and it nearly drowns him.

Likewise, man's knowledge of good and evil is a sort of "magic." He can know good now only alongside the possibility of the evil which he *imagines;* and everything he imagines he can also "make happen" in a sort of magical way. Nothing earthly is beyond his ability to fashion or destroy. Retaining God's image in himself as a sub-creator, he becomes with his purloined "knowledge" the abuser and manipulator of God's creation; he can twist every good thing, make or destroy beauty, pervert, dominate, manufacture things both great and terrible. "And the LORD said, . . .

'Nothing that they propose to do will now be impossible for them'" (Gen. 11:6). Man can build Babel with almost a "magical" hubris. To give more up-to-date examples: he can imagine and create the Internet for mass communication, and make the vilest pornography available to millions through it, ruining countless lives and human relationships; he can "imagine" splitting the atom, and "magically" incinerate whole populations anywhere. He has "direct experience of the knowledge of good and evil," and because of this "the creation was subjected to futility" (Rom. 8:20). By the sixth chapter of Genesis, God is even said to be sorry he ever made man. "The LORD saw that the wickedness of man was great in the earth, and that every imagination [*yetser,* meaning "impulse, urge"] of the thoughts of his heart was only evil continually" (Gen. 6:5).

The "unclean spirits" are related to all this in a mysterious way. We see this "personal" evil outside of Eve's mind in the Garden in the form of the serpent, but by his speech he breathes the thought into her mind to taste the fruit. Later, we find "sin" personified in the striking warning that God speaks to Cain, who will nonetheless go on to commit the first murder (thus unleashing a multitude of "evil breaths" that have poisoned the human imagination and the whole world ever since): "Why are you angry, and why has your countenance fallen? If you do well, will you not be accepted? And if you do not do well, sin is couching at the door; its desire is for you, but you must master it" (Gen. 4:6-7). The image is that of a lurking beast, a demon, the devil. The language here in this early chapter of Genesis resembles another, much later warning, that of 1 Peter 5:8-9: "Be sober, be watchful. Your adversary the devil prowls around like a roaring lion, seeking some one to devour. Resist him, firm in your faith. . . ." Whether it is a chthonic demon-beast, or sin, or the devil — whatever it is called, it is always something outside seeking to "get into" the human imagination.

THE GOSPELS PRESENT US with the image of Jesus Christ, the Word made flesh, the Last Adam. What we see in him is the God who transcends "the knowledge of good and evil" and has divine power over it. He cures illnesses, casts demons out with a mere word and sends them into the abyss, calms the storm, raises the dead, crucifies in himself the sin of the whole world, and finally overcomes death itself. He is the One in whose image we are intended to be conformed. He brings the Law, with its ethical demands, to its completion, so that by learning to live in his Spirit, we are no longer victims of a "knowledge" — a direct experience — we cannot handle, but are set free by grace to be transformed into his likeness (cf. Rom. 7 and 8). "In Adam" we die as victims of our knowledge of good and evil; but "in Christ" risen from the dead, we are made alive by participating in God's "Breath" (see 1 Cor. 15:22, 45).

Returning, then, to the meaning of "unclean spirits," we can think of them as those countless multitudes of evil thoughts and suggestions that play on the human imagination, that plant in us the seeds that grow into all the ills of individual and collective human existence. Not only do we do battle with our own passions and thoughts from within, but we also face the "unclean breaths" that are in the very "atmosphere," so to speak. "For we are not contending against flesh and blood, but against the principalities, against the powers, against the world rulers of this present darkness, against the spiritual hosts [*ta pneumatika,* meaning "the *breathly* beings"] of wickedness in the heavenly places" (Eph. 6:12). Again, if all we hear in this sort of passage is the mythology of a bygone era, then we have not really heard it at all. The battleground is the mind, and this is a warning to us, regardless of the age in which we live, that we are constantly assailed by ideas, images, suggestions, pressures, misconceptions, misperceptions, mendacity, propaganda, lies, slander, and so on. These things are everywhere, in the very air we breathe.

The passage quoted above continues with the famous list of items of spiritual "armor" to be worn by the inner man (Eph. 6:13-17). The equipment is, of course, meant for the interior battlefield, and what is being protected from the phalanxes and flank attacks of "unclean spirits" is the imagination and the mind. The verse immediately following brings us back to our constant need for prayer: "Pray at all times in the Spirit [Breath], with all prayer and supplication. To that end keep alert with all perseverance . . ." (Eph. 6:18).

For what, then, in our practice of prayerful stillness and measured breathing, are we seeking? First of all, we are continually beseeching God for his Breath of life, his Spirit. Luke 11 provides for our reflection here. In verses 24-26, Jesus says, "When the unclean spirit has gone out of a man, he passes through waterless places seeking rest." (Here we find the notion mentioned earlier that the desert fathers would later take so literally: that unclean spirits inhabit the wilderness.) "And finding [no rest]," Jesus continues, "[the spirit] says, 'I will return to my house from which I came.' And when he comes he finds it swept and put in order. Then he goes and brings seven other spirits more evil than himself, and they enter and dwell there; and the last state of that man becomes worse than the first."

The problem for the man in the parable is that his inner being — his "house" — has been emptied and cleansed of the unclean spirit, but nothing has come in to fill the emptiness left behind. If left empty, there is nothing to prevent "evil breaths" from re-entering and occupying the same interior space. A few verses earlier, however, teaching on the subject of prayer, Jesus had already specified what it is for which his disciples should pray to fill that vacuum: "Ask, and it will be given you; seek, and you will find; knock, and it will be opened to you. For every one who asks receives, and he who seeks finds, and to him who knocks it will be opened. . . . The heavenly Father [will] give the Holy Spirit to those who ask him!" (Luke 11:9-10, 13).

This is the way out from being the victim of the knowledge of good and evil. It is the Holy Spirit who raises us above the realm of unclean spirits, so that we can draw close to God. It is "grace," and it is above mere ethics and legalisms and traditions, above the law itself, since these cannot ultimately raise us beyond the influences of evil. Rather, law by its very nature as a corrective measure keeps us operating within the limits of the knowledge of good and evil. Its function is to clarify these things, and — good as the law is as a corrective measure — it serves only to bring us to the realization that we need something that transcends this lower level of mere laws and justice. "Christ is the end of the law" (Rom. 10:4), "for the written code [of the law] kills [i.e., punishes], but the Spirit gives life" (2 Cor. 3:6).

So, in prayer we entreat the Holy Spirit, asking and seeking and knocking, that he might fill our imaginations and minds, banishing every evil thought and influence and the unclean breaths that surround us.

chapter 8

The Mind

*The understanding, like the eye, whilst it makes
us see and perceive all other things, takes no notice of itself; and it requires art and pains to set it
at a distance and make it its own object.*

John Locke, *An Essay Concerning
Human Understanding*, 1.1

The battleground of "unclean spirits" — unclean
mental "breaths" — is the mind. This is not the
same thing as "the brain," of course. The ancient Hebrews located the thought life — the reason or intellect, the emotions and passions, the good urge and
the evil urge, and so on — throughout the human
body. Thoughts might emanate from "the heart" or

84

"the kidneys," and the deep emotions and unruly passions came — so it was believed — from the location of the intestines. Although we no longer imagine the mind-body connection existing in such a thoroughly anatomical way, the truth is that we still are almost clueless as to how the mind and brain interact.

Although physicians long ago "located" the mind in the brain, researchers remain baffled by the latter. The brain is the most complex organ — indeed, the most complex "thing" — we "know" of, and we simply do not "know" it very well at all. Does the brain "generate" the mind, or does the mind "operate" the brain, or some combination of the two? If the mind — or consciousness — "operates" the brain, how are we to make sense of that? Numerous documented "out-of-body" and "near-death" experiences (NDEs) — the latter frequently occurring in clinical settings — suggest such a seemingly wild and implausible idea, with the mind still processing sense data such as hearing and seeing while it is supposedly "unconscious." In such cases the mind is somehow taking in sensual information even while disconnected from the organs of sense themselves. Persons who have been in these states accurately describe sights and sounds they "should" have been unaware of while unconscious, tell of looking down on their own bodies, moving into adjacent rooms, and so forth. For the strict materialist, this sort of report can only be disturbing, like Marley's ghost showing up on Christmas and upsetting Scrooge's conceptual applecart. Where the brain-mind connection is concerned, regardless of the materialists' wishes for a neat physical explanation for the mind's existence, the jury is still out and looks to be for many years to come.

The value of the ancient Hebrew model, therefore, lies not in its scientific veracity, since we know the mind works through the brain and not, say, the kidneys. Yet, in its identification of the whole body with the mind or consciousness, it reminds us that more than the brain is connected to the mind; one's total physical being is. In Jewish thinking, in fact, the body and the soul (*nefesh, psyche*) are a single entity, even if a distinction can be made between them as "parts" of a unified whole. In New Testament language, when the physical body and soul are separated in death, there is still a "spiritual body" — a "resurrection body" or "inner man/nature" waiting to be "clothed" with immortality — through which the soul and consciousness will continue to exist. It is the Spirit or Breath of God that will insure this continued existence of the person. "He who raised Christ Jesus from the dead will give life to your mortal bodies also through his Spirit which dwells in you" (Rom. 8:11). One need only read St. Paul on the matter to grasp this Jewish-Christian perspective of the connection of body and soul. (See, for example, 1 Cor. 15 *passim,* and 2 Cor. 4:16–5:5.)

Thus, for Paul, what is necessary is for us to be, as he terms it, continually "renewed" (*anakainosis,* meaning "made new again"): "Though our outer nature is wasting away, our inner nature is being renewed every day" (2 Cor. 4:16). ("Outer" is, in Greek, the word *exo,* and "inner" is *eso.* Therefore, when the distinction is made between "exoteric" and "esoteric" in religion and spirituality, this is what is being differentiated. The most important aspect of religion is hidden from sight in this life: it is "esoteric." The external forms of religion are intended only to aid what is essentially unseen and internal. This might even be said of Holy Communion: "transubstantiation" doesn't just end with the significant change from bread and wine into Christ's body and blood, as if the goal is to create a "holy object" outside and independent of us. Rather, the transformation continues in our reception of it in a "transubstantiation" of our "inner nature." The twenty-fifth of the Anglican "Thirty-Nine Articles" is absolutely correct to insist that the sacraments "were not ordained of Christ to be gazed upon, or to be carried about, but that we should . . . worthily receive the same." The exoteric exists only for the esoteric.)

Our "inner nature" is to be identified with the mind [*nous*], that is to say, our consciousness — the "self" that lies beyond our ego or identity in this short earthly life (see Chapter Six above). Paul refers to the "inner nature" that must be "renewed" as the "mind" in Romans 12:2: "Do not be conformed to this age but be transformed by the renewal of your mind." And, in fact, this follows and fills out his injunction in the previous verse: "Present your bodies as a living sacrifice, holy, acceptable unto God, which is your reasonable service [*logiken latreian*]" (Rom. 12:1, KJV). Body and mind, in other words, must be operating in harmony with each other — the body must be directed toward God along with a constantly renewed consciousness. This is, as Paul puts it, "reasonable service."

Likewise, this is what St. Mark the Ascetic was also getting at in the passage quoted in Chapter Five: "The mind cannot be still unless the body is still also; and the wall between them cannot be demolished without stillness and prayer." To put it succinctly: The goal is to *unite* our bodies and minds in prayer, knocking down the barriers between the two by practicing stillness and interior attentiveness, so that we can be "renewed every day" — transformed — by the experience of God's Breath within. What we do with our bodies both in prayer and in daily living should be conducive to furthering our spiritual life. Our minds and bodies are meant to be working together, functioning harmoniously. Going back to the language Abba Moses used with John Cassian, this is the immediate goal in our practice of asceticism. At the very least, without this inner-outer, body-mind harmony, we will fall short of an adequate prayer life.

Thus I offer three points regarding our minds and spiritual practice:

First, in line with what was said in the previous chapter, "the knowledge (direct experience) of good and evil" is primarily at work in our *minds:* what we *imagine* within ourselves we can often bring into concrete existence. The "unclean spirits" — those evil suggestions constantly "breathed" into the cultural atmosphere surrounding us — may influence us from without; but it is the corresponding "evil thoughts" deriving from our own disordered passions (*epithu-*

mia; see Chapter Two above), which these outside influences conceive within us, that add to the world's already enormous heap of countless evils. This sort of "mind" is referred to sometimes in Scripture as "the old self," or "the flesh" — in other words, that which is *dying* or *dead* in us if "we have been crucified with Christ": "We know that our old self was crucified with him so that the sinful body might be destroyed" (Rom. 6:6). "Therefore, if any one is in Christ, he is a new creation; the old has passed away, behold, the new has come" (2 Cor. 5:17). "Put off your old nature which belongs to your former manner of life and is corrupt through deceitful lusts [*epithumia*], and be renewed in the spirit of your minds, and put on the new nature. . . ." (Eph. 4:22-24). Such texts remind us that there is *something in our minds* that was crucified with Christ, and *something in our minds* that is being renewed in the Holy Spirit: the former is "the old man/self" who is passing away with his "body of death"; the latter is "the new creation" or "the new man/self" who possesses a "spiritual body" that will know resurrection in Christ.

Second, the Law — either that of Moses or that as manifested in the universal laws and regulations of mankind — is not the answer to our renewal of mind.

Law exists only on the level of "the knowledge of good and evil" in order to provide us with a "diagnosis" of our condition. As was noted in the last chapter, it cannot raise us to union with God, who alone has power to "renew" us. If law is only a diagnosis of the mind, what we need is a capable Physician who can mend it: no diagnosis ever cured anyone — only the healing powers of someone trained in the skills of healing. Speaking in paradoxical language, therefore, Paul writes that the good, but inadequate, Law is met by another "law" within ourselves: "the law of sin." "So I find it to be a law that when I want to do right, evil lies close at hand. For I delight in the law of God, in my inmost [*eso*] self, but I see in my members another law at war with the law of my mind and making me captive to the law of sin which dwells in my members" (Rom. 7:21-23). What is necessary is a mind that can transcend the level of law and "the knowledge of good and evil" altogether, along with that of sin and slavery to the passions. This, of course, is what our spiritual life is meant to do, transforming our consciousness and consequently our behavior from deep within. For us to be healed in mind, we are meant to become "holy," flowing naturally with the Spirit of God (cf. 2 Cor. 3 *passim*); we are not meant to be white-knuckled, scrupulous, worried rule-keepers, attempting to save ourselves with nothing but a written diagnosis in hand. "That which is born of the flesh is flesh, and that which is born of the Spirit is spirit" (John 3:6). "God is spirit, and those who worship him must worship in spirit and truth" (John 4:24).

Third, part of our prayer life is precisely to allow for distractions from within. Although distractions are what we seek to overcome, we can't do that by trying to tackle them directly. They become tar babies for us if we try to confront them. The more we try to push them away, the more they will stick to us. That may sound very wrong at first, but it is in fact one of the aspects of prayer we must undergo if transformation is to occur within our selves. Our minds operate on at least two levels simultaneously. In the prayer of stillness, breathing in and out rhythmically, we repeat the words of our prayer in our minds (perhaps the Jesus Prayer or some other invocation of God). While we are doing that, we will undoubtedly experience the inner chaos of our passions and thoughts. Rather than becoming disturbed and worried by them, though, we simply continue the prayer, but *observe* the thoughts that arise from within. One level of consciousness is "with Christ," and from that vantage point we look down upon the other, that of our own thoughts and feelings, watching what recurring things particularly disturb us. These are the areas that Christ the Great Physician is curing. Here there can be no application of external "rules" — we have reached the place within where there is utter unruliness. This is also where the Spirit will bring his peace, felt sometimes for a brief period, maybe longer, until we are taken up and swept over the chaos once more. But, while we are applying this contemplative practice within the depths of the mind, Christ is at work putting to death our old self, raising up the new, forming out of the disorder of our interior chaos a new order of creation, and doing all this while we abide in stillness and breathe.

chapter 9

Invocation of the Name

God be in my head,
And in my understanding.

Sarum Missal

"Whoever calls on the name of the Lord shall be saved" (Acts 2:21). When Peter, citing the prophet Joel (2:32), proclaims these words in the first post-Easter apostolic sermon, it is certainly the case that what he means by "the name of the Lord" is the name of Jesus. This emphasis on the unique power of Jesus' name is underscored in the two subsequent chapters in Acts, where Peter also is recorded as saying that the lame man outside the Beautiful Gate of the Temple was healed by Jesus' "name, by faith in his name" (3:16), and still later when he declares before the Jewish rulers, elders, and scribes that "there is no other name under heaven given among men by which we must be saved" (4:12).

Early Christians called on the name of the Lord Jesus for salvation, for rescue from their ills, temptations, sins, and death. To call on Jesus' name was, in fact, to call on God — "God with us," "God reconciling the world to himself in Christ" (Matt. 1:23; 2 Cor. 5:19). For the Christian to call out, "Lord, save me!" (Matt. 14:30), as Peter is said to have done as he began to sink when attempting to walk on the roiling waves with Jesus, was to call on both the man Jesus and the invisible God simultaneously. The two were intimately associated: to call on the Son was to call on the Father. And this points us in the direction of what "calling on the name" of Jesus still means for us who practice it in our prayers today.

To invoke the name of Jesus is to invoke the God revealed by Jesus. Whereas "God" — in the nonspecific and multiple senses which that term conjures up within our individual minds, philosophical and religious systems, and diverse cultures — can be experienced and known beyond the bounds of the specific revelation of Christ, it is regarded by Christians to be the case that the fullest possible "knowledge" of God is finally relative to the incarnational criterion he established in Jesus. For many, "God" is the invisible and ineffable, not necessarily a "he" or anything identifiably "personal," more a felt presence or an indeterminate sense of awe: the ultimate, the mysterious, the "force" that binds the universe together (to risk echoing the language of *Star Wars*). "God" — if we even can use the term legitimately here — is encountered as "something" that is not a "thing" among things at all, but that which encompasses and holds together all contingent things — the *Tao,* perhaps, or the otherwise nameless *Logos.* "God" is intuited, felt, and understood as being the supreme Beauty, the absolute Truth, the ideal Good. If conceived of as personal, God is the One "in whom we live and move and have our being." Beyond all the lesser gods there is "God," and what God is cannot be comprehended, only encountered in the mystery of existence.

Closer to home, in the faith of Israel, God is he who gives the Law, who calls a people and forms them and cleaves to them in covenant love, and who speaks by the prophets. The Christian believes that this same God has gone even further in manifesting himself. He has assumed the flesh of Israel ("Salvation is from the Jews" — John 4:22) and made himself known face-to-face in Jesus of Nazareth. To call on *this* name, then, is to leave all ideas of divine anonymity behind once and for all, to move from the *hearing* of the ears to the *sight* of God condescending to walk among us to bring us Good News. There is no question but that we have moved in Jesus decisively from any notion of a (safely?) "non-personal" God to a very definitely personal and interactive God, one who looks at us through human eyes and unites himself fully to our human condition. We even go so far as to believe he has taken on himself our sins and death and overcome them both in himself. From this point on, we conclude, we know God specifically as "God, the Father of our Lord Jesus Christ" (Col. 1:3), a designation that contains in itself a rich wealth of content distinctive to the faith of Christians. In other words, this is an identifying marker that sets God as revealed in Christ apart from all other ideas and images of who or what God might conceivably be. Once he is identified with Jesus, we see him in contradistinction to numerous other posited identities. What we understand by God is now what we see in Jesus.

The Gospel of John stresses the invocation of the name of Jesus in prayer. In the Farewell Discourse (chapters 14-17), Jesus makes his essential union with the Father plain: "He who has seen me has seen the Father" (John 14:9). In other words, the Father is *invisibly* and transcendently — in his "character," if one might be permitted to use that word in an imprecise way here — what Jesus is *visibly* and palpably in human dimensions. So it is that he can say later in the same discourse, "Truly, truly, I say to you, if you ask anything of the Father, he will give it to you in my name. Hitherto you have asked nothing in my name; ask, and you will receive, that your joy may be full" (John 16:23-24). Still further, in his prayer to the Father, Jesus seems to suggest that his name is bound with the Father's own name: "I made known to them thy name, and I will make it known, that the love with which thou hast loved me may be in them, and I in them" (John 17:26). The "name" of God which Jesus the Son makes known, according to John, is possibly "Father" (corresponding to his use in addressing God — unusual within his own culture — of the familiar word for "father" in Aramaic, *Abba;* cf. Mark 14:36; Rom. 8:15; Gal. 4:6). Perhaps this is John's answer to Agur's mysterious question: "Who has ascended to heaven and come down? . . . What is his name, and what is his son's name?" (Prov. 30:4). Even more likely in the case of this particular Gospel, it is the divine name "I Am" to which Jesus refers. Repeatedly in John, Jesus identifies himself by the phrase "I Am" — for example, "Before Abraham was, I Am" (John 8:58). This self-appellation is undoubtedly a reference to the "name" of God as revealed to Moses at the Burning Bush (cf. Exod. 3:13ff.), the paradoxical name that is really not a name, which became (so it is argued) the basis for the Tetragrammaton in the Old Testament, YHWH (possibly meaning "He Is"). This name was considered so frighteningly holy by the Jews that it was never pronounced, except each year by the High Priest in the Holy of Holies in the Temple on the Day of Atonement. (It has always been noteworthy for Christians that the name "Jesus" — "Yeshu," "Yeshua," "Yehoshua" — means "YHWH saves.")

Again, all this for the Christian comes back to the definitive revealing of God as bound to the person and message of Jesus of Nazareth. To call out "Abba, Father!" or to invoke the One who is "I Am" is to identify God in the light of Jesus himself and his teaching. Conversely, to call on the name of Jesus is to come likewise to the Father, whom Jesus himself lovingly called "Abba," to the One Who Is, revealed in the Law and the Prophets and the Writings of Israel, and finally in the Gospel. And, turning to the Gospel of Matthew, to invoke the name of Jesus is to know also "the name [singular!] of the Father and of the Son and of the Holy Spirit" (Matt. 28:19).

Over the course of centuries, the tradition of invoking Jesus' name has taken various forms. The Jesus Prayer of the Christian East is one notable practice, made famous many decades ago in the West by the translation of the nineteenth-century Russian devotional classic *The Way of a Pilgrim.* (One might recall the discussion about this little work and the Jesus Prayer in J. D. Salinger's 1961 novel *Franny and Zooey*). In turn, *The Way of a Pilgrim* ignited an interest in such Eastern Christian writings as those collected in *The Philokalia,* and over time the Jesus Prayer has become familiar to believers from all the Christian traditions.

The Jesus Prayer is an elaboration of that most essential of prayers (the one that in fact secretly underlies every prayer we utter, including the Lord's Prayer), the *Kyrie eleison* — "Lord, have mercy." It goes like this: "Lord Jesus Christ, Son of God, have mercy on me, a sinner," or "Lord Jesus Christ, have mercy on me," or "Lord Jesus Christ, have mercy" — and there are still other variations. The heart of the prayer is, of course, the name of Jesus. It is prayed traditionally with the body relaxed, usually in a seated posture, with the head bowed, and along with the rhythm of one's breathing. The mind remains focused on the words of the prayer, repeated either vocally or mentally. In time, the Prayer becomes habitual, and practitioners of it over a long period — and I can testify to this myself — may even discover it "praying itself" deep within and even during one's sleep.

Even in the West, simply praying the name "Jesus" has long been practiced, often by itself with no elaboration. Among those in the West who emphasized such prayer, several stand out. The name of Jesus was celebrated powerfully in the fifteenth homily of St. Bernard of Clairvaux's *Sermons on the Song of Songs*. Devotion to the name of Jesus was strongly promoted by the Franciscans (one thinks of St. Bonaventure, for example), and most strenuously in the fifteenth century by the Franciscan "Apostle of Italy," St. Bernardino of Siena. In Western devotion even the *Hail Mary* centers on the name of Jesus, not on that of Mary, his name (as also hers) being added to the biblical texts from which the prayer was taken (cf. Luke 1:28, 42).

Having all this in mind, we should be careful not to see in the name of Jesus some sort of talisman or charm, or interpret the words of Jesus in John 16:23-24, to the effect that we receive whatever we ask in his name, to mean that anything we want may be ours if we just "use" his name. On the contrary, we cannot "use" the name of Jesus any more than we can control God. To invoke the name of Jesus is to dispense with all such manipulative devices, to swear off all magical thinking, to reject anything even remotely suggestive of a "name-it-and-claim-it" religion. It is an act of reliance and trust, a submission of our wills to his will for us (which is to transform us into his likeness).

The corrective word to those who might think that Jesus' name has quasi-magical or talismanic properties is written for us in 1 John 5:14: "And this is the confidence which we have in him, that if we ask anything according to his will he hears us." The operative phrase here, of course, is "according to his will" — and indeed, to call on the name of Jesus is precisely shorthand for "Thy will be done." It is an act of abandonment to him, a statement of faith and trust. It says in effect, "I don't know what you have in store for me, but whatever it is, I accept and receive it from your hand." It may be difficulty, it may be great pleasure, it is always the unexpected — but God, Jesus promises, gives his children "good things" (Matt. 7:11), even in the midst of the many pains and disappointments inherent in this transitory life. What we need are eyes that recognize them when they're given. Particular "good things" that God provides may be what we really have longed for all along, though not in the cherished forms of our fantasies. They may entail sacrifice or renunciation, because what is truly "good" is always worth the death of what is lesser — such as comforts, acquisitions, personal plans, and even personal associations. Praying the name of Jesus opens us to all such possibilities, and more besides; it is to break through the gray walls we build around ourselves, to place ourselves in an open, horizonless expanse so broad and wide as to overwhelm. This is no magical, manipulative formula, but a submission to the One who already has our true destiny in his sovereign hands.

Lastly, to invoke the name of Jesus means that we are ever seeking to know him better. We should be exceedingly cautious about expending any time or energy on those who purport to be visionaries or spokesmen of what God is supposedly "newly revealing" today. To say it straightforwardly, we don't need new "private revelations" and "secrets" allegedly given in apparitions to cloud our minds. We can do without visionaries and hearers of locutions, and do just fine. Even if some "private revelations" and claims of apparitions are harmless or interesting phenomena in their own right, as far as our spiritual lives are truly concerned, we simply don't need them. Nor should we pursue them with anything beyond mild and detached curiosity, no matter how sensational they appear — perhaps the more sensational they are, the more we should avoid them altogether. This is a word of caution that has been repeated by the most revered spiritual teachers of our tradition, from the desert fathers through St. John of the Cross and into our own day. The sensational is a distraction from the real work of prayer.

Three related accounts from the sayings of the desert fathers will suffice here, perhaps, to illustrate the point. Once, one story goes, a monk saw a vision of an angel of light who announced to him, "I am the angel Gabriel, and I have been sent to you." The old man replied, "Check and see whether you were sent to somebody else. I'm not worthy to have an angel sent to me." And, at that, the demon vanished. Another time, we're told, the devil showed himself to a monk and said, "I am Christ." The old man just shut his eyes. "I am Christ," the devil repeated. "Why are you shutting your eyes?" The monk replied, "I will see Christ in the next life." Another time a demon asked a monk, "Would you like to see Christ?" The old man responded, "A curse on you! I believe Christ when he said, 'If anyone says to you, "Look, here is Christ," or "Look, there is Christ," do not believe him.'" And the demon vanished. Such tales have a profound lesson to teach: keep focused on the sober-minded path of discipleship.

Recourse to the teachings of Jesus and the Scriptures are sufficient for his disciples. Other great spiritual texts, serving as "midrash" or sound exegesis of Scripture, are entirely beneficial for us as well, as we will see in the next chapter. Study should occupy a central part of our spiritual lives, and it is primarily through the practice of attentive application of our minds in this way that we gain deeper, authentic knowledge of God. This has always been the essential, irreducible piety of both Jews and Christians. Those who invoke the name of Jesus are meant to be listening to him daily, listening with the interior "ears" of the heart. Then, when we call on his name, our prayer will encompass the content of all that.

chapter 10

Study, the Bible, and Reading

Blessed Lord, who hast caused all holy Scriptures to be written for our learning: Grant that we may in such wise hear them, read, mark, learn, and inwardly digest them, that by patience, and comfort of thy holy Word, we may embrace, and ever hold fast, the blessed hope of everlasting life, which thou hast given us in our Savior Jesus Christ. Amen.

Thomas Cranmer,
The Book of Common Prayer,
Collect for the Second Sunday in Advent

Study, the Bible, and Reading

My library is my garden and orchard.

Judah Halevi, Jewish poet,
philosopher, and physician (c. 1075-1141)

Marcel Proust wrote that reading is "that fruitful miracle of a communication in the midst of solitude." Reading, of course, doesn't happen only in solitude. It is central to our corporate liturgies, for example, in which the Scriptures are read aloud. The written word can be a civic communication that forms communities and ratifies covenants (see, e.g., Exodus 24:7-8 and Ezra 8:1-8). It can be the substance for a broadcast or some kind of public entertainment or numerous other things. But Proust's observation reminds us of the peculiar power that reading in solitude can possess. It can be a "fruitful miracle" when something read and "inwardly digested" changes us from within, even though the transforming thought came to us from without.

Solitary reading requires close attention, a slow pace in order to absorb, and an interaction that might be helped by having a pencil in hand for our own annotations and reflections — be they to highlight and stress a notion or to rebut one. Solitary reading, assuming it is serious reading, opens our minds to the minds of others; new ideas are formed, philosophies are shaped and altered, attitudes and behaviors are challenged. Sometimes in such close reading, as perhaps in no other context, we discover ourselves engaged in a living dialogue that spans centuries and the globe: we may find ourselves having, say, an inner discussion with a Greek or Chinese thinker of the fourth century before Christ, or with some English poet of the seventeenth century A.D.

To read in solitude is, too, the main staple of Christian spiritual life. It has been this way ever since the beginning. Christians took from their roots in Judaism a special reverence for the sacred Scriptures and an earnest commitment to study. It is our legacy from the rabbis through our Jewish apostles, carried on by the fathers of the church, and becoming central to the Christian monastic heritage; and it establishes the firm basis for all Christian thought and experience down the millennia.

The literate Christian solitarily pondering the written word of God, or some carefully written exposition of it, is, it must be emphasized, engaged in what arguably could be the most fundamental act of prayer: listening for God's voice to speak from the text to his or her heart. All prayer from our side is a response to God's word. All too often we mistake prayer as our attempt to get God to respond to *us;* but prayer is the reverse of that. It is our response to the God who is not silent but always, graciously, initiating the conversation with us. His word is accessible, a sign to us of his condescension and care for us. In communion with it we pray to him.

God accommodates himself to our level by speaking to us in a sort of "baby talk." This "baby talk" is what we find in the Scriptures. The reformer John Calvin, who held a very high view indeed of the Bible's inspiration, nonetheless used this very same humble analogy: "As nurses commonly do with infants, God is wont in a measure to 'lisp' in speaking to us. . . ." He continues by saying that, although such "lisping" as to infants doesn't "express clearly what God is like," it succeeds in bringing some knowledge of him to us according "to our slight capacity." "To do this," writes Calvin, God "must descend far beneath his loftiness."[1] Calvin here is simply stating a truth that Christians have always held: that the Bible is *a means* toward knowing God experientially. He condescends

---

1. John Calvin, *Institutes of the Christian Religion,* Book I, XIII, 1.

to us through its human words and lifts us from it to a deeper consciousness of his presence. It isn't an end in itself.

Thus, regarding the importance of reading the Bible, the fourth-century church father St. Jerome could write to a friend, "I beg of you, my dearest brother, to live among these sacred books, to meditate upon them ceaselessly, to know nothing else, to seek nothing else" (Letter 53). Of St. Francis of Assisi, whose love of books was never very great, his biographer St. Bonaventure could nonetheless write, "Although he had no skill in Sacred Scripture acquired through study, his intellect . . . probed the depths of Scripture with remarkable acumen. . . . Where the scholarship of the teacher stands outside, the affection of the lover entered within."[2] Or, again, as Abraham Joshua Heschel, the great twentieth-century Jewish scholar and activist, expressed it, "The word of God is as vital to [the pious man] as air or food. He is never alone, never companionless, for God is within reach of his heart."[3] Such statements as these remind us that the

2. St. Bonaventure, *The Life of St. Francis of Assisi* (Rockford, Ill.: Tan Books, 1988), Chapter 11.

3. Abraham Joshua Heschel, *Man Is Not Alone: A Philosophy of Religion* (New York: Farrar, Straus & Giroux, 1979), Chapter 26.

reading of the Bible is primarily grounded in God's love for us and our proper response to his bending toward us in such a humble and human way — through the means of fallible human authors, using human words, written in human languages, and inscribed on impermanent earthly material.

That being said, two caveats are worth noting here. First, the term "the word of God" is not simply synonymous with Scripture, but inclusive of it. For the Christian, drawing on the language of the Fourth Gospel, it is synonymous ultimately with Jesus Christ himself, "the Word of God" who "became flesh." The written word — the canon (literally, the "measuring stick") of Scripture — is read in light of him. Conversely, Jesus is himself understood in light of the revelation made to Israel as recorded in the Hebrew Bible, the Old Testament. The Old Testament is, for the Christian, understood in relationship to Christ (see Luke 24:27, 32, 44-45; John 5:39). He is the fulfillment of it. He stands in relation to what was set down in the Old Testament as "the body" stands in relation to the "shadow" it casts (Col. 2:16-17; cf. Heb. 10:1). He is the substance, the visible and palpable form that was foreshadowed in the sometimes obscure forms of the Old Covenant. He is the "goal" of the

Mosaic Law (Rom. 10:4). More than this, he provides the definitive corrective (the "hermeneutical" or "interpretive" key) to various notions contained in the Old Testament, which, gathered together as a single sacred canon, is the product of centuries. And, while it embraces a number of perspectives within the purview of its collected texts, nonetheless without Jesus it falls short of the most explicit revelation of God's "character." So it is, for example, that Jesus can say repeatedly and straightforwardly in the Sermon on the Mount, comparing his own corrective and complementary message to what is contained in the Law and the Prophets, "You have heard that it was said. . . . *But I say to you . . .*" (Matt. 5:21-48, emphasis mine). He says this after stating to his disciples, "Think not that I have come to abolish the law and the prophets; I have come not to abolish them but to fulfill them" (Matt. 5:17). Yet his fulfilling of them includes an authoritative critique of them, and, indeed, at times a revision.

So it is that when we refer to both the Old and New Testaments as the word of God, we do not mean this in fundamentalist, absolutist, or literalistic terms. We always read the Bible as that which witnesses to Jesus, pointing beyond itself to him and thus to God.

It is never opaque or an end in itself; it is a window onto Christ, a threshold over which we pass into the presence of the One whose "word" it is.

The second caveat is that spiritual reading does not preclude reading beyond the Bible, the canonical word of God. The more confident we are of our own rootedness in our Scriptures and tradition, the more we find the freedom to let our reading expand to include even what might not, on the face of it, appear to be Christian spiritual reading at all. Reading is always "spiritual" in some way, whether it's done well or poorly (a "miracle," to use Proust's language), because we are endowed with spiritual minds. All our reading makes an impression on our thoughts and so forms us in one way or another. But, so long as at the center of our routine is a daily, meticulous reading and an ongoing, lifelong re-reading of Scripture, other texts we include in our practice of spiritual reading over the years will be incorporated into and fully imbued with our personal living dialogue with God.

Spiritual reading is defined not so much by *what* we read (apart from our reading of the Bible — which should remain our one constant), but by *how* we read what comes to our attention. Do we read "with God" or mentally apart from him? Assuming the former frame of mind is our own, and that God is ever present and moves us "from behind," so to speak, we can relax in the belief that some books reach us throughout our lives that are not merely reflective of our own taste. The Spirit blows where he wills, and often it's a book he's wafted our way. Frequently it's a text we would not have chosen for ourselves, but somehow it has grabbed our attention and won't let us go — and the result of going along with that "capturing" of our attention and actually reading the text may well be a positive and important change in our lives we hadn't seen coming or could have imagined.

Obviously, some discernment is called for, and unquestionably not every book that comes our way is good for us. But, if we continually place our emphasis on what's central in our spiritual study and apply our minds primarily to that, we will discover that our capacity for sound discernment will develop. God's universal truth, as such fathers as (for example) Justin Martyr, Clement of Alexandria, Jerome (on his better days), and Augustine realized, can be heard even in the writings of pagan philosophers and poets — something attested to by Paul, as well, in Acts 17:28. It might be mixed up with some questionable thoughts and ideas that need to be assessed by the "measuring stick" of the biblical canon, but the well-grounded, literate Christian can learn how to distinguish between the true and the doubtful. So it is that Justin Martyr in the second century could write that "those who lived reasonably [within pagan cultures] are Christians, even though they have been thought atheists; as, among the Greeks, Socrates and Heraclitus, and men like them . . ." (*First Apology,* xlvi). In a similar vein, Augustine could write two centuries later in his *Retractions,* "What we now call the Christian religion existed among the ancients, and was from the beginning of the human race, until Christ himself came in the flesh; from which time the already existing true religion began to be styled 'Christian'"(I, xiii, 3). Such views as these are no doubt surprising to some — both to Christians and to non-Christians alike — who would regard Christianity as narrow-minded and self-contained intellectually; but they reveal that the well-read early Christian could learn how to eat the fish and not choke on the bones of a non-Christian text. We can learn this, too.

Perhaps one additional caveat is called for, and that is the pressing practical matter of time. We live in an age when — because of our technologies — we find our days, hours, and minutes crammed with constant busy-ness. We are racing from our beds in the morning to our beds at night, and the whirl of our activities in between leaves us little time for meaningful reflection. How are we supposed to read seriously, then? How are we expected to give this activity sufficient time?

While this dilemma is a real one, the truth is that we can carve out of our days *some* time for reading and prayer, and we should make the effort. Perhaps practical necessities won't permit us the time to read in all the areas I will suggest below, but we can do *some* reading in the most important areas at least. We can do so consistently, methodically, and earnestly, and still have time to do whatever the day's demands require of us. Often it is the case that we fill our time with lesser pursuits. We need relaxation, certainly, and entertainment within reasonable limits can be beneficial to us; but if these push out all time for spiritual reading, then we need to recognize this as a form of mental sloth and reset our priorities accordingly.

*   *

We can perhaps picture our spiritual reading "plan," then, as a series of five concentric circles. Think of each successive "circle" as surrounding the one(s) before it, giving a "context" to each of the circles it contains. The two most important circles are the one at the center and the one immediately surrounding the center. We will explore all of them briefly, one at a time, but let me begin by identifying the "five circles," moving from the center to the periphery. The first circle includes the Bible and those commentaries and aids that help us to understand the text. The second circle includes spiritual writings from our own expansive tradition: the works of theologians, prophets, and thinkers of all ages (Eastern and Western, patristic, monastic, medieval, Reformational and Counter-Reformational, modern and post-modern, and so on). This includes the classics and contemporary Christian thought as well. (One thinks of C. S. Lewis's regimen of reading five "old books" to every new one.) The third circle includes a broader reading in world religions, philosophy, psychology, world literature, history, and the sciences. The fourth circle includes an even broader reading in current news of the day, as well as those "worldly" philosophers, journalists, and intelligent challengers of religious belief. The fifth and final circle includes light reading, when needed.

If at least three out of these five categories seem

less important and less "spiritual" to us, then we need to see that our most important reading (that which we do in the first two, central categories) is not to be done in a vacuum, but within the living context of history, the arts, the sciences, philosophy, other religions, and the world around us. What we do in solitude is never unconnected from the world, as if religion is escapism or a mere refuge. Rather, we "think by means of the revelation," as the Russian Orthodox theologian Vladimir Lossky wrote somewhere; and our *thinking* is precisely what is being transformed through our reading. If we are "escaping" anything at all by our faith in God, it is the constraints of narrow thinking, of not recognizing the expansiveness of thought that we have in God. By stressing the first two categories (the Bible and tradition), we become anchored; our thoughts deepen as they plunge into the wonder, awe, and wisdom of God. These are our stays and supports, and the knowledge we gain there is inexhaustible and inwardly transfiguring. So, even if the other, contextual "circles" of our reading are "less spiritual," they become "more spiritual" as we bring to them what we have gained from our most vital reading. Let us, then, look at the circles individually.

The first circle: the Bible and those commentaries

and aids that help us to understand the text. Enough has probably already been said about this above, so I will add only the following. We read the Bible as we do any other book, with a critical eye and with an inescapable awareness that we now read it in a modern context. We should seek to understand it in light of the best contemporary scholarship. It is useful to know the original languages, but that's certainly not necessary for the average reader. There are numerous Bible-reading aids and tools to make up for what is not known firsthand (study Bibles, commentaries, concordances, lexicons, atlases, and so on), and the reader should not shy away from putting intellectual effort into his reading by utilizing these. God's word is certainly breathed into the Scriptures, but it came by way of human agency and within specific historical, cultural, and linguistic contexts. It's invaluable to learn such details, and also to read the Bible (especially the Old Testament) as the records of a *developing* understanding of the revelatory God. If we read it as a book that has within it various viewpoints that are in tension, we will see that an evolution of understanding the very character of God is growing throughout the canon. (To give but two examples of tensions within the Old Testament: There is an intellectual struggle between the conventional retributive "punishment and reward" morality of Proverbs and the later unconventional viewpoints expressed in Job and Ecclesiastes. Similarly, the narrow and legalistic stance taken toward foreigners among the Israelites visible in the book(s) of Ezra and Nehemiah is countered by the gracious and expansive attitudes toward foreigners affirmed in the latter portion of Isaiah, as well as in the books of Jonah and Ruth.) Jesus is the One who brings the Old Testament's developing understanding of God's revelation into sharp focus.

The second circle: the spiritual writings from our own expansive tradition: the works of theologians, prophets, and thinkers of all ages. The Christian tradition is wide and broad and deep, and it contains a vast array of insights and reflections on the central truths we have in Scripture. Eastern and Western, patristic, monastic; Catholic, Orthodox, Oriental, Anglican, Protestant, Pentecostal; ancient, Byzantine, medieval, scholastic, Reformational and Counter-Reformational, modern, postmodern — all these and more are included in our extensive tradition. The broad-minded contemporary Christian will not be suffocated and imprisoned by a single expression of his larger heritage, but will seek (as he does with the Bible) to know the many tensions, interplays, and ideas that make up the full Christian intellectual universe. Just as one should be immersed in the Bible but not become a mere biblicist, so the Christian who wishes to have a larger vision of God's revelation should engage as much of the whole tradition and its various perspectives as he can, and not settle for becoming just a traditionalist in only one intellectual stream. This is not to say that one shouldn't settle into one tradition as his spiritual home, but only that one should — in genuine Christian charity — seek to understand and appreciate even those points of view that challenge his comfortable positions. A Catholic should try to understand the mind of Luther; an Orthodox should be able to appreciate why a Calvin or a Milton or a Bunyan have their place among the classics of Christianity; a Protestant should endeavor to appreciate Catholic and Orthodox devotion to Mary; and so on. The narrower one's spiritual viewpoint within the faith, the less possibility he has to hear God's still small voice, his warnings and his corrections. A broad reading within the full tradition is a spiritual discipline that prevents the individual Christian from simply being led by the nose into others' disputes (usually outdated and frequently based on misunderstandings and calumny of "the other side"). Most conflicts within Christianity are unnecessary; and reading is one positive way to recognize that sad fact. And, of course, the benefit of spiritual reading is that it deepens our prayer and transforms our lives.

The third circle: a broader reading in world religions, philosophy, psychology, world literature, history, and the sciences. Learning to appreciate other religions and their sacred texts, as well as world mythologies, is worthwhile for those who (as with Justin, Clement, Augustine, and others, as mentioned above) wish to place God's revelation in the context of man's overall religious awareness from primitive times to the present. World religion is not a threat either to the truth of revelation or to the particularity and uniqueness of Christ. Rather, it shows that mankind has a perennial openness — ranging from the most animistic to the most sophisticated expressions — to the transcendent. It is something that has universally characterized the human race and always will. Christianity appeared not in a void, but among things earthly, amid the many human cultures and their myriad searches for truth and for God. This is its larger context. Likewise, no Christian should avoid knowing what he can of the humanities and their disciplines. If it is "human" or about his creation in any way, it is God's concern; and we can be enriched by engaging the ideas and insights of the ages. Jesus didn't fear sitting down at table with anyone; and we shouldn't fear sitting down at table (so to speak) with the world's many philosophers and scientists and poets and psychologists — even the atheistic and agnostic ones — to gain perspectives and to investigate concepts that may very well shape us and deepen us.

The fourth circle: an even broader reading in current news of the day, as well as those "worldly" philosophers, journalists, and intelligent challengers of religious belief. Karl Barth said he studied the Bible with it in one hand and the newspaper in the other. C. S. Lewis didn't stay so closely in touch with the daily news. Still, Lewis did interact in print with thinkers and theologians, pundits and professors, and numerous others popular in his day. Since we do not live in a vacuum, we should know what is having an impact on our world here and abroad. Knowledge of current events (*not* including celebrities' lives!), political or medical or scientistic challenges to common virtue and faith, new trends in philosophical thinking, the directions being taken in popular culture (often indicated by current entertainment) — all these are worthy of a Christian's attention. Even the monk and the hermit live in the modern world and have a responsibility to engage it in the name of Christ. Our faith is Incarnational, and we understand the Resurrection to be cosmic in its consequences for the material order. In other words, this world, its unfolding history, its integrity, its materiality — all have meaning to God. He "loved the world" and came "not to condemn it, but to save it." Our reading should include a concern for that which is ultimately God's.

Lastly, the fifth circle: light reading. Sometimes we simply need to read something humorous or something that brings us pleasure or a sense of adventure. G. K. Chesterton read and wrote detective stories, for example, as did Ronald Knox and Dorothy Sayers (all brilliant apologists for Christianity). Lewis wrote the Narnia books and the Space Trilogy. There is ample pleasure and fascinating theology in the supernatural thrillers of Charles Williams. All this is simply to say that "fun" reading can be spiritually beneficial. Nor should we confine lighter reading to only the works of Christian writers. God is not opposed to laughter or pleasure or even a bit of escapism, and there is no need to think that perpetual seriousness is a mark of godliness. It isn't. We often need a boost and mental relaxation, and light reading is good mental health, and good mental health is also good spiritual health.

We live in a day when it is said that the book is a thing of the past, that it will disappear as new visual technologies replace it. Whether or not that will happen remains to be seen; but reading as a discipline will not become outdated. Even if it is done with a small electronic, handheld device instead of a bound volume, solitary reading will continue to be a "fruitful miracle." For the spiritual life, it will continue to be foundational and essential.

THERE IS ANOTHER "book" that we should spend time with, however, one not printed, one which is wordless. We live in this "book" every moment of our existence and always shall. It "speaks," but we cannot hear its voice. Referring to its various contents, the psalmist says, "There is no speech, nor are there words; their voice is not heard; yet their voice goes out through all the earth, and their words to the end of the world" (Ps. 19:3-4). It is "the book of creation" (as medieval writers used to refer to it), or nature; and next we turn to its role in our spiritual lives.

chapter 11

Nature

*You never enjoy the world aright, till the Sea it-
self floweth in your veins, till you are clothed
with the heavens, and crowned with the stars;
and perceive yourself to be the sole heir of the
whole world, and more than so, because men
are in it who are every one sole heirs as well as
you.*

Thomas Traherne,
Centuries of Meditations, I.29

*The stuff of the universe, woven into a single piece
according to one and the same system, but never
repeating itself from one point to another, repre-*

126

sents a single figure. Structurally it forms a Whole.

Pierre Teilhard de Chardin,
The Phenomenon of Man

A part from God, all things, visible and invisible, are his creation. From the perspective of God, then, they are made, fashioned, formed, and directed; they are contingent in their being on the sole Being that is not contingent. He alone knows what creation includes beyond our material senses, why and how it exists, and he alone comprehends it in such manner that its origin and goal, like the knowledge of good and evil (see Chapter 7 above), are ruled and contained.

Comparatively, we human beings scarcely have little more understanding of these things than do polliwogs or pigs. To us, our knowledge appears impressive; to the infinite mind of God, it must seem barely above the cognitive level of the primeval fish-brain from which our far more complex brain is physically descended. In no way is that meant as a denigration of mankind's high status among the other earthly creatures, or as some sort of denial of our being "made in the image and likeness of God." It is merely a reminder that we have only begun our journey as a species and as a race, that we exist in time really just an instant past the Beginning. We have much more to know yet, much more to become by God's grace. Eternity stretches endlessly ahead of us, and there God already is.

If to God all else that is, is his "creation," to us it is "nature." *Nature* derives from a Latin word meaning "birth," and we are born in and through nature. We are part of it, above it only in that we are aware of it and consciously responsible for it in a way very definitely far removed from those polliwogs and pigs. What to God seems barely above the bestial — our human uniqueness and inborn *imago Dei* — to us seems (quite rightly) immensely separated from even those primates most closely related to us genetically. Between ourselves and God is the infinite difference between the created and the Uncreated; between us and the other animals is a gigantic (but tiny compared to our ontological and epistemic distance from God) gulf of awareness.

We are of nature, natural, born of the soil of earth, a point made by the ancient mythic picture of God fashioning man of the clay. We are, then, nature itself, nature that is self-aware, conscious, and conscious — most importantly — of meaning and of God. We divine that there is meaning in nature; we believe that this meaning is found only in God. Furthermore, as Christians, we believe that God has bridged the ontological chasm between our nature and his through the Incarnation of the Word. Through him God will ultimately be realized as "all in all" (1 Cor. 15:28).

Nature, then, must play a significant role in our spiritual lives. The Hebrew mind, unlike the Greek mind, perceived that nature apart from God was incomplete. The Greek mind tended to view nature as a self-contained *cosmos* — ordered and normative. For the Jew, nature was God's creation, and human beings were both part of it and stewards of it. *With* the rest of nature, not just as a creature set *over* it, the Jew looked at the incompleteness inherent in all things and in the direction of the One who governs all things in his ineffable knowledge. God had made what evidently was still not fully finished, still incoherent to reason, still troubling, violent, unpredictable, inconclusive, chaotic; but it was seen as that which could also be entrusted to the purposes of the Creator who originally had made it good and would decisively steer it on to its perfection. The Hebrew mind would trust God, then, even in the face of human evil and natural catastrophes, knowing that what was imperfect in the world through the inroads of disorder would in God's time be rectified. Man, in this view, does not stand dismayed before the obvious disarray of an essentially good creation; rather, he cooperates in partnership with the Creator in a covenant to bring order to natural and human affairs.

As Christians, then, more Hebrew than Greek in mind, we do not look at nature to sentimentalize or idealize it like the nineteenth-century Romantics tended to do. Nor do we see it in utilitarian terms, as simply a storehouse of resources for our exploitation and pleasure, as the worst examples of technology and science have done. We neither adore it nor plunder it. Nature is ourselves, and we stand among and with the other creatures, facing God, who alone completes nature and gives it meaning. We are meant to be stewards, accountable for what we know.

Like St. Francis of Assisi, we can and should address the other creatures as "brother" and "sister." We should also acknowledge, simply from the science of evolution if from nothing else, how utterly interconnected our existence is to everything in nature. We sum up in ourselves a progression of life spanning many billions of years from protozoan form, through piscine existence in the oceans, to existence on the land, as creatures with upright gait and intelligence. To God, this is merely one movement, like the first brief movement of an unfinished piece of music; to us, it is an unimaginably vast expanse of time. With the creation we move toward the Creator, and in Christ the Creator embraces everything in heaven and on earth and brings us to himself (see Col. 1:15-20; Eph. 1:20-23; also Rom. 8:18-25; 1 Cor. 15:27-28).

When we pray, we can find in nature a source of purity and spiritual nourishment. It is, as God deems it, "very good." Sometimes we should stop and observe the trees, mountains, fields, water, stars, the animals, the sounds and sights — all from the hand of God, not made by man, not really *ours* at all. We shouldn't be pantheists, certainly, nor should we — like Gnostics or mystics of a gloomy and morbid temperament — despise nature and seek to shut our senses to its "allurements." Neither tendency is healthy or sane. God gave us materiality, he gave us bodies and sensuality, he gave us eyes and ears and noses and touch, he gave us the occasional spine-tingling sense of the existence of unseen presences, and these things should be neither worshipped nor shut out. Prayer allows for open eyes and appreciation of nature. It allows us to recognize both the frailty and the glory of what God's imagination has made, to wonder at the developing and unfolding of myriad forms of life, to see with the mind the magnificent cascade of an endlessly bursting divine creativity and variety that stretches on into a universe of incalculable proportions. Even if all we do is stand alert to a leaf moved by the whisper of a breeze, in gratitude for simply existing right then and there, we have prayed perfectly in that instant. It's necessary that we recall, like the poet Joyce Kilmer, that "only God can make a tree."

If our prayer lives are then transformed into action, as they always ought to be, we will begin to see that nature is in our keeping through a covenant with God. Like all covenants, this one can be, and frequently is, horribly violated. How, then, should we exist with all our creaturely "brothers" and "sisters," all of whom have been "reconciled to God" by the Incarnation, Resurrection, and Ascension of the Word-made-flesh? Practically, what should be our covenant with the creatures of God? Do they exist solely for us? No, they exist for God, and what "use" they are to us is surely limited to what is humane; and what is humane is defined by the compassionate humanity we see in Jesus.

Lastly, whatever meaning we have, whatever meaning our own lives possess, whatever meaning we discover in prayer, this meaning is intimately associated with the nature of which we are — and ever shall be — a part. We really have no meaning except as it relates to our original status as stewards of God's good creation.

chapter 12

Psalms

Be filled with the Spirit, addressing one another in psalms and hymns and spiritual songs, singing and making melody to the Lord with all your heart.

Ephesians 5:18-19

O f all the books of the Bible, it is the Psalms that focus most on the individual person. For thousands of years they have been sung or said corporately, in the Jerusalem Temple and in all the synagogues throughout the world, in church and monastery and open fields, on land and on sea. They are the hymns of Israel and of the Kingdom of God, the *vox sponsa* — the voice of the "spouse," which is collectively the people of God. But the Psalms are also the hymns, prayers, and laments of individual believers. The vast majority of texts in this ancient hymnbook have to do with the singular "I."

Think of the opening lines, for instance, of Psalms 3 through 7, which are typical of many of the psalms. Each opening line before that of Psalm 8, which breaks the pattern, is singular: "O LORD, how many are my foes!"; "Answer me when I call, O God of my right!"; "Give ear to my words, O LORD; give heed to my groaning"; "O LORD, rebuke me not in thy anger, nor chasten me in thy wrath"; "O LORD my God, in thee do I take refuge; save me from all my pursuers, and deliver me. . . ." Each psalm is a *cri de coeur,* passionate and intended to elicit a response. It is the utterance of someone who will not settle for God's silence, who makes demands, who is not content to suffer in stoical fashion. The psalmists want recognition, redemption, and restoration. In short, they want justice and implore mercy. Sometimes they give voice to anger and self-justification, and invoke curses on the heads of their enemies and terrorizers. Every human emotion — pleasant and unpleasant — finds its expression openly made before God in the Psalms. The psalmists — God bless them — spill their guts, vent their spleens, cry in pain, rejoice and praise and laugh, question God, challenge him, remind him of promises apparently forgotten, and usually seek to draw him into the conflicts and confusion of human life.

It is a good thing that solitary souls learn to pray the Psalter, and pray it over and over. In so doing, we soon discover that every thought and emotion can be spoken to God from our depths. Before we even begin to see in the Psalter its Christological dimension (consider, for example, the Anointed Son of Psalm 2, the suffering and pierced righteous man of Psalm 22, and the reigning Lord of Psalm 110, as well as other instances), it is worth our noting the book's earthiness and honesty. Perhaps some of the raw emotions displayed there we cannot ourselves comfortably pray as Christians — the notorious outcry of Psalm 137:8-9 comes immediately to mind (although the monastic tradition "spiritualized" this into a metaphor meaning that the shattered "little ones" in the text were our seedling sins, dashed against the "rock" that is Christ before they ever had the chance to mature — quite a hermeneutical stretch, admittedly, but it kept the monks' consciences quiet). Still, even a psalm like 137 reminds us that God can hear and receive our anger and ugliest wishes — that he can listen even to our bitterest and most biting feelings.

The tendency we have sometimes is to think that piety is made up of warm feelings and beautiful ideas. Prayer, however, is not "thinking lovely thoughts," having warm fuzzies, pursuing goose pimples, or dwelling on sentimental and saccharine imagery. The majesty of God is never glimpsed in a pastel-hued holy card or a Thomas Kinkade cottage. This is a form of idolatry we need to eschew. Prayer is for people who see life as it is, with all its aches and angst, its glories and grace, its sorrows and satisfactions. People can — and should — pray in the face of grief, anger, betrayal, divorce, poverty, illness, violence, terror, catastrophe, and just plain sheer evil. They should also praise and give thanks for — if nothing else — the privilege to exist, and their ability to understand at least enough to be amazed by that remarkable fact. Even more, they should acknowledge God, and thank him for the love he has shown in his sovereign acts; and — moving along even further into the Christological dimension of the Psalms — thank him for the Son and Suffering Servant who has identified himself with us, entering into our sorrowful world to rescue us and put us back onto the royal road. The solitary one who cried, "My God, my God, why hast thou forsaken me?" (Ps. 22:1) is the same to whom we, in solitude, pray the Psalms.

If we are looking for a "school of (vocal) prayer," we can do no better than to pray each day the Lord's Prayer, the Jesus Prayer, and portions from the Psalter. However we do this, however we arrange our schedules to accommodate the practice, and whatever other prayers we may add, these three prayer forms are most beneficial to us. With the Lord's Prayer we pray the words Jesus taught us — a good, succinct, short, basic prayer that hallows God's name and covers our essential daily needs. With the Jesus Prayer — or just invoking his name — we enter into the mystery discussed above in Chapter 9. With the Psalms we shape our hearts and minds in such a fashion that we become free before God to speak in an authentically human way to him. No need to hide ourselves behind pious sentiments and flowery devotions. The Psalms teach us to speak from the heart in a straightforward and unashamed manner. God knows our hearts, our passions, our desires, our sins, and our frustrations. We don't need to pretend with him. We can voice these things openly, and he can take it. He's large enough to embrace *all* that we are.

If we can do this and see in the Psalms just such a "school" for existential prayer, we can also begin to see how bringing out before God all the thoughts of our hearts allows them to be cleansed and purged and healed. Perhaps we can pray our own psalms to him as well, modeled on the real and vibrant example we find in these ancient hymns. And if sometimes the old psalms disturb us, all the better it is for us. Genuine spiritual life requires the soul's disturbance; and the neat status quo and fine categories of our lives and prejudices should be shaken and tumbled down before the living God. The Psalms force us to face him and cry to him; and they force us to listen for him as well.

chapter 13
....

Knowledge and Love

_Love never ends; as for prophecies, they will pass
away; as for tongues, they will cease; as for knowledge, it will pass away. For our knowledge is imperfect and our prophecy is imperfect; but when
the perfect comes, the imperfect will pass away.
When I was a child, I spoke like a child, I thought
like a child, I reasoned like a child; when I became
a man, I gave up childish ways. For now we see in
a mirror dimly, but then face to face. Now I know
in part; then I shall understand fully, even as I
have been fully understood. So faith, hope, love
abide, these three; but the greatest of these is love._

1 Corinthians 13:8-13

This quotation of Paul's quite unaffectedly inter- weaves the corporate perspective ("*our* knowl- edge"; "*we* see") and the personal perspective ("when *I* was a child"; "now *I* know in part"). In the first chapter of this little volume, I likened the per- sonal spiritual life to an emergence out of a darkly wooded world into the brightness of a larger vista. Each of us, I maintained, is a solitary soul; but to- gether we are solitary souls in communion with one another. More than that, we believe we share one Spirit in Christ. Perhaps that is an indication that at a profound level of our selves we participate in a common, unitary, but variegated consciousness as well. It has never been demonstrated by science, it should be stressed yet again, that our own con- sciousness originates in the brain. Rather, it is quite possible that our personal consciousness — the most basic and most mysterious aspect of our men- tal experience, a reality we usually merely accept un- accompanied by self-awareness or speculation at all — somehow "uses" the brain. Perhaps, then, made in "the image and likeness of God," we are more "in- terconnected" than we realize.

Both science and religion agree that we share a common ancestry, and this has been expressed from ancient times by conceiving of humanity as making up a single social "man" — a single "body." St. Paul carried this concept into Christianity, one familiar to him from the interpenetrating cultures he knew first-hand, growing up as he did during the intellectual and cosmopolitan golden age of the city of Tarsus. Thus he could write that Christians are made "members" of "the Body of Christ" through baptism (cf. especially 1 Cor. 12). So, individually we are "members," and together — "corporately" — we are one; one in Christ's Body, one in sharing his Spirit-Breath.

But our spiritual lives are solitary, and our ascent to "truth" is necessarily individual. Everything pondered in this book has been presented here only to *suggest,* to provide thoughts for mental *rumination,* to *indicate.* I have purposely avoided anything too dogmatic or ideologically constrictive, believing that Christianity at its best is a dynamic movement of faith in the direction of God. Dogma, to be valid in religion, serves only to indicate what lies beyond words, never being an end in itself. Dogmas and doctrinal abstractions are no more real than physics equations are "real" — it's the universe that is real, not the equations that help us make sense of it. Christ's yoke of discipleship is something lived and experienced. It's not primarily a batch of theological "equations," definitions, and precise formulations. The word *dogma* itself is derived from the Greek word *dokein,* which means "to seem." The word implies, therefore, that a "dogma" is not an end in itself. It is a flat reflection only of something else that is substantial and greater by far. We require understanding, of course. We need to involve our reason, we need the theological "equations" from time to time, but doctrinal formulations provide us with ways of understanding what we already *are learning to know by experience.* They aren't *real.*

One of the curious facts of the supposed war between science and faith is that what is really happening is an opposition between two competing dogmatisms. This row has been going on now for nearly two hundred years. But genuine science cannot in fact oppose faith. It hasn't the means to do so, since *the object* of faith lies beyond the competency of empirical science. "Science" (a term that, it seems to me, is presumptuous when used as an inclusive — dogmatic? — singular) cannot pronounce on what may, in fact, come from a different mode of perception than that utilized by the empirical scientist.

However, the aberration of science that has justly

been called "scient*ism*" by C. S. Lewis and others can oppose what it believes to be "faith." "Scientism" is simply the long-standing assumption that all true knowledge comes through the senses, is empirical, and can be observed and experimented upon. It is convinced of its own thoroughgoing materialism. There is no other form of knowledge than the empirical; "God" is a term for a superstitious, nonexistent projection of ourselves, and no more rational a hypothesis than fairies or talking mules. "God" as a viable concept is dogmatically and doctrinally refused, spirituality is — at best — a species of psychological phenomena, and religion is most likely an evolutionary by-product. What this kind of "scientist" thinks of "faith" is rather obvious — it's essentially an irrational sentiment, bolstered (especially in the cases of the most successful world religions) by clever, self-serving, rationalistic systematizers of theology; but it's all stuff and nonsense, and theology is a non-science, utterly devoid of any "true" knowledge.

Sadly, nothing so misrepresents a truly scientific curiosity than this sort of rigid and blinkered worldview. Science, one would imagine, should display an interest in at least the possibility that the empirical method is not the only method for ascertaining what might be real. Surely there might be other, parallel ways of knowing — and reality is far more expansive than any single methodology could ever possibly handle. It would be a good thing for such scientists and the latest flock of pop-atheists to read William James again (if ever they read him before, which is doubtful). Here was a scientist who faced exactly the same mentality as their own in his day. Certainly no one would accuse James of being an orthodox, dogmatic Christian; but he was justifiably skeptical of the whole "scientistic" mind-set. In 1907, in his book *Pragmatism,* he could write,

> I firmly disbelieve, myself, that our human experience is the highest form of experience extant in the universe. I believe rather that we stand in much the same relation to the whole of the universe as our canine and feline pets do to the whole of human life. They inhabit our drawing-rooms and libraries. They take part in scenes of whose significance they have no inkling. They are merely tangent to curves of history the beginnings and ends and forms of which pass wholly beyond their ken. So we are tangent to the wider life of things. But, just as many of the

dog's and cat's ideals coincide with our ideals, and the dogs and cats have daily living proof of the fact, so we may well believe, on the proofs that religious experience affords, that higher powers exist and are at work to save the world on ideal lines similar to our own.[1]

"The proofs that religious experience affords" are what we discover in the practice of faith and spiritual life, and they can't be known by the dogmas of "scientism" or even of religion. The old, post-Constantinian dogmatism of Christendom, the sort that insisted on "right belief" to the point of enforcing it with physical and mental punishments and (in some ages) worse, is — thankfully — mostly gone. Sometimes we forget that among the charges laid against Jesus, for which he was nailed to a cross, was one more or less along the lines of "heresy." It is an abominable fact that those who have served "orthodox" systems bearing Christ's name have killed and tortured for the preservation of those systems, contrary to the clear teachings of the Lord himself. Too often it has been "dog-

---

1. William James, *Pragmatism* (New York: Library of America, 1988), Lecture VIII, p. 619.

mas" that have been "protected" by violence (true of secular dogmas every bit as much as the religious ones) — abstractions preserved by brutalizing living human flesh. When dogmas are used to keep persons in the herd, under control, dominated or patronized, then they are being used wrongly. If they assist us in grappling intellectually with what "religious experience affords," fine. If not, they are useless and even, on occasion, harmful to us. The goal of faith is not to grasp the "truth" of this or that dogma. The goal is to arrive at the knowledge and love of God, and dogmas are signposts along the side of the main road.

So let us conclude this little primer by reflecting on those words of Paul quoted at the beginning of this chapter. The key words are "love" and "knowledge" (or "understanding"). Paul says that "love never ends." Our ascent to God is the response we make to God's descent to us in Christ. It is not a matter of our having perfect knowledge of God — that isn't possible in our present state of consciousness. "Our knowledge is imperfect" (a warning to every dogmatist!); indeed, "it will pass away." Why? Because we are heading in the direction of what will be "perfect" (*teleion,* meaning "complete," "end," "goal," "mature"), and that will be an ontological or existential state. "When the perfect comes, the imperfect will pass away."

Paul thus compares our spiritual life to personal growth. Here he switches, as noted above, to the first-person singular: "When I was a child, I spoke like a child, I thought like a child, I reasoned like a child. . . ." He is referring to our time here now, our lives in the present of growing up into the knowledge — the experience — of God. It is a bit more hopeful than William James's simile of our being in the universe in the way that dogs and cats inhabit our homes, but the meaning is not all that different. What we think we know will be challenged as we grow up: we will be changed; our minds will not remain forever in their infantile state. This is true of our natural lives, and it is true of our spiritual lives as well. Faith undergoes transformation, and our assumptions and ideas about God will constantly be stretched and altered. We won't remain children forever if we constantly seek to know God. And this will happen in each of us individually: "When *I* became a man, *I* gave up childish ways."

Paul contrasts our present condition with that which is to come by the analogy of a mirror. In ancient times, mirrors provided far more distorted and hazy reflections than they do today. What is seen in Paul's spiritual "mirror" is — if you will — the features of God. Looking within, into our hearts, or looking without at the creation, we see a dim reflection of that which cannot be seen directly. Perhaps the mirror might also be our doctrines and dogmas, when seen for what they are and, at their most polished, at their best. But God's reflection we see "dimly." What and who God is remains mostly obscure. Even Jesus, who reflects him perfectly, is beyond our sight. We know him by his "presence," but it is not tangible; we sense him in the ineffable, in nature; we hear him in the sacred texts; we glimpse him in stillness and in the words of familiar psalms. The mirror is dim; "I know in part" only. I bear the yoke, trusting in the destination; but I do not see it yet.

The promise is this: We will finally arrive. At some point we will emerge from the prolonged birth canal of this life, through which we are passing now. We will emerge into the full light of real life, newly born. Our old nature is withering away; our inner nature is being renewed daily (see 2 Cor. 4:16). The seed of our earthly bodies will "die" and be planted, and from that outer shell will spring the "spiritual" resurrection-body (see 1 Cor. 15:42-50). Then, as Paul says, we will see God "face to face." More than that, we will see that our knowledge, so limited and confined now, so tiny and "childish," will give way to an expansive understanding that we cannot yet conceive: "I shall understand fully." And, more even than that, and once more suggestive that the potential of our consciousness far exceeds the mechanism of the brain, "I shall understand fully, *even as I have been fully understood.*" We will see as God sees, sharing his knowledge, his own illimitable view.

Finally, says Paul, whereas faith and hope will no longer be needed, giving way to vision, love alone will endure. Paul would no doubt understand and affirm the insight of St. John: "God is love" (1 John 4:8). There is nothing sentimental here. What is meant is that "knowledge" is nothing at all unless it is experiential and unifying. "Love" (*agape*) refers to participation, giving, sharing, communion. It is that which bonds us to God because God bonded himself to us, becoming what we are, undergoing our death, taking responsibility for our sins, and — through the resurrection and renewal of the Spirit — uniting our lives to his.

Our dogmas say as much; but it is "the proofs that religious experience affords" that take us to the heart of the matter. In the end — and we have in fact arrived at the end of this small book — it is the experience of bearing the yoke of Jesus that will provide the proofs we need of the truth and goodness of the Christian way. It must become a habit, though, a routine, a practice, a real taking upon oneself of the disciple's life to gain the proofs; and those proofs will be chiefly the recognition of a transformation that has occurred within oneself, usually over a period of years. Jesus' yoke is "light" — he doesn't demand absurd austerities; he doesn't glorify suffering or self-hatred. His toughest appeals were challenges to take on self-discipline, under the guidance of his teachings; and also the call to stand committed to the way of his Kingdom even when the world around his disciples presented numerous different ways. Gloomy self-negation was not part of his summons.

Lived as intended, life under Jesus' yoke is what gives "rest" to our souls — not greater stress, not increased guilt, not self-nagging, and certainly not dread of God and everlasting death. It is a life of increasing knowledge and love, pragmatically and enthusiastically lived, with eyes wide open to the world and all its peoples. The yoke of Jesus means learning, within a pragmatic "school" of thought and experience, how to live fully now and always. And that yoke has been, if you will, the burden of this book.